(Continued from front flap)

dependence from human dominance as long as the marshes remain in marshy condition. Marshes comprise their own form of wilderness. They have their own life-rich genuineness and reflect forces that are much older, much more permanent, and much mightier than man."

This important book, endorsed by leading conservationists,* is filled with an abiding love of the out-of-doors, and the wisdom of a mind that, for all its detailed, scientific knowledge, is yet warmly human and humble.

H. Albert Hochbaum has made twenty-two vivid drawings to illustrate the book.

*"I don't know when I have ever read anything that so beautifully analyzed and expressed the richness and variety that is such an integral part of the wildlife of wetlands . . . One obtains a picture of marsh wildlife from a man who has undoubtedly studied it more deeply and with greater understanding than any man who has ever lived."—Richard H. Pough, Conservationist

Other books by Paul L. Errington

MUSKRAT POPULATIONS — "This comprehensive book, with its detailed cataloguing of muskrat populations in a variety of habitats in Iowa, must be indispensable to other workers . . . reveals Errington as an outstanding field naturalist."—*Journal of Applied Ecology*.

OF PREDATION AND LIFE — ". . . packed with valuable and fascinating accounts of predation, predominately among the vertebrates. . . . Thirty-two sketches, many of them full page, supplement the excellent text."—*Science Books.*

Iowa State University Press
Ames, Iowa 50010

*of men
and marshes*

Illustrated with drawings by
H. Albert Hochbaum

# of men
and marshes

Paul L. Errington

THE IOWA STATE UNIVERSITY PRESS • Ames

QH
87.3
.E7

To the memory of

ARTHUR KARR GILKEY, Ph.D.

Boulder, Colorado, September 25, 1926
Mount Godwin-Austen, Pakistan, August 10, 1953

To a man of civilized ethics, manners, and scholarship, yet one who loved wilderness, too.

To a man of self-direction and discipline who loved freedom, too.

To a man of strong friendships who loved solitude, too.

To a man who loved the natural out-of-doors, whether of marshes or of mountains, for itself and for its own values, for its drama of the living and the non-living, and for the peace that it gave him.

To an admirable man and a beloved friend.

preface

This writing deals with those wetlands known as marshes and, particularly, with those natural marshes occurring over the glaciated prairies of north-central United States and adjacent Canada.

My own experience with glacial marshes started with muddy feet on the family farm in east-central South Dakota. It continued through years of hunting and fur-trapping and through the long-term research programs that accompanied and followed my rather erratic evolution from a professional trapper to a biologist and college professor.

I have seen and lived among the plains and mountains of the West and the coniferous forests and open lakes of the North, and I know some of the great scenic areas of our continent. These I love, too, yet for me, as an individual, no other natural feature has ever had the enduring attraction of an undespoiled chain of marshes in an undespoiled setting of glacial hills.

Feeling as I do, it is hard for me to understand the willingness of the public to drain marshes even if the land so drained might produce corn or some other profitable agricultural crop. Monetary profit should not be the sole objective for land use. We need corn-fields and economic bases for our civilization, but we also need marshes where they may be said to belong.

The wise ancients, in writing that man does not live by bread alone, doubtless had in mind something similar to what I have, though I do not know that they valued marshes as part of their cultural surroundings. Very possibly they did not, and they may have had reasons not to, for some marshes have meant big problems at some times for some peoples. At any rate, the ancients recognized that there should be more in human experience than making a living.

•   •   •

The National Wildlife Federation, in announcing the theme for National Wildlife Week for 1955 as "Save America's Wetlands," called attention to the tremendous losses of wetlands that have occurred in the United States since settlement by the white man. Of the more than one hundred and twenty million acres of marshes and swamps originally lying within our boundaries, less than a fourth remain fit for use by waterfowl and other marsh life. Most of the loss has been through artificial drainage.

As expected, the duck hunters and the fur trade gave support to programs for the maintenance and restoration of marshes as our wetland resources declined. More, however, is involved in a positive attitude toward marshes than striving to increase ducks and musk-rats—though ducks and muskrats undeniably belong in the picture. I believe that marshes could add greatly to human enjoyment if more people really knew them the year around. I believe that there would be more interest in marshes if more people appreciated how interesting and beautiful marshes are as marshes.

Greater familiarity with marshes on the part of more people could give man a truer and a more wholesome view of himself in relation to Nature. In marshes, life's undercurrents and un-knowns and evolutionary changes are exemplified with a high degree of independence from human dominance as long as the marshes remain in marshy condition. Marshes comprise their own form of wilderness. They have their own life-rich genuineness and reflect forces that are much older, much more permanent, and much mightier than man.

contents

1. *of glacial marshes and time*

Earth has had its great climatic changes, its alternate advances and withdrawals of continental glaciers. Because of their recency, the evidences of Pleistocene ice sheets are conspicuously before us. Of the recognized glacial stages in North America, the latest, known as the Wisconsin, left some of the modern glacial marshlands of southern Manitoba, western Minnesota, northwestern Iowa, and the eastern Dakotas.

Prairie potholes and shallow sloughs and lakes with rush-grown fringes and bays, remnants of immense lakes lying in sandy or peaty or muddy or salty flats, waters of rocky moraines, waters surrounded by tamarack, spruce, white cedar, willow, alder, aspen, oak, waters surrounded by sedge and grass, waters covered by cattail, reed, bulrush, burreed, waters full of waterlily, pondweed, coontail, bladderwort, arrowhead, marsh waters over hard rock or soft muck—these we have where the ice made dams, big dams or little dams.

Wherever the ice sheets or the loads they carry obstruct drainage, there impoundments occur. Wherever ice sheets come and go, there we shall have renewed conditions for the formation of glacial marshes. As long as there be plants and animals adapted for living in marshes and as long as there be impoundments suitable for them to live in, this long may we expect the phenomenon of marshes, glacial or otherwise, to persist.

The over-all phenomenon of glacial marshes has been involved with Life for a long time, and, being linked with fundamental forces of the universe, will presumably continue for some time to come. It does not follow that the marshes of the future will retain all or even most of the plants and animals that we associate with the marshes of today. Changes may be expected that are quite independent of human intervention.

One winter day, I was working over the drought-exposed bottom of a marsh in north-central Iowa. At the surface of the peat, I saw the fore part of a small skull facing me. I gently dug it out with a knife, thinking that the specimen would interest my mammalogist colleagues but not expecting that it would be described in the National Museum as a new species of Pleistocene otter. Its nearest relative now lives in western Mexico, far from our otterless interior of Iowa!

Whatever that marsh may have been when that otter lived, or whatever kinds of other animals may have lived there then, the remains of a long-dead otter hint of continuities extending far beyond the short spans of human civilizations.

Yet, the identity of a glacial marsh is subject to geologically rapid change. Ernest Thompson Seton recounted an Indian legend in which the sun god assigned the muskrat to the "between-land" —that which is neither land nor water. As "between-land," a marsh represents a stage in the filling of a lake or pond with silt and vegetation, and, as the filling continues, the marsh tends to disappear. We might consider the duration of a marsh, individually, as but a geological moment, with moments recurring over and over again to produce geologically ephemeral new marshes.

The advent of modern man as a geologic agent has hastened the filling in of many glacial marshes. Indirectly, through his acceleration of soil erosion, he has brought about a premature filling even of marshes he has intended to preserve. Dust-laden air and silt-laden waters are not peculiar to the era of human domination, but they have become increasingly characteristic of it.

In a separate category from man's incidental effects on glacial marshes is his purposeful drainage. During my life, I have seen two major drainage movements in the glaciated north-central prairies.

One of these movements occurred in the first two decades of the century and took marshes that could be drained relatively cheaply and easily. It took the then-drainable ponds and marshes of

the richer farmlands and many extensive marshy areas that offered, or seemed to offer, opportunities for agricultural development. The second movement gained impetus in the forties and was largely centered upon the Minnesota and Dakota potholes that previously had been too expensive or difficult to drain.

To one who loves marshes, the end effects of drainage are the same, in that marshes cease to be marshes, whether they turn into weed patches or cornfields. If we look for variations, we are more apt to find them in the details of pre-drainage enterprising, in what people say or do in order to contribute to the objective of getting marshes drained. There may be publicly owned wetlands, in plain view of someone who might profit from promoting drainage, someone who might profit from the drainage engineering, someone who might profit or hope to profit from working the drained land. Perhaps application of political pressures may be needed to make

of glacial marshes and time   3

everything legal. Or, it may only be that someone has a little rush-grown duck pond on his property, and, if he wishes to drain it, nothing less than the laws of physics may prevent him from draining it.

And technology has found so many loopholes in the laws of physics that marshes formerly considered undrainable are now drained with the expectation of their long staying drained. Ditches are machine-cut to depths of fifteen feet or more through one glacial knoll after another, and, in these ditches, capacious tiles are laid and covered up so that soon all looks as before except that the marshes are gone. Nor, in areas having electric power and big pumps to take out the water, do the drainers even have to show the deference to gravitation that they once did.

Of course drainage, as a work of man, does not have complete permanence. Despite technology, there are ditches and tiles that may become so choked that, if man does not actively interfere, drained lands may again become marshes. Or marshes may be intentionally restored, as has already happened in the United States and Canada, sometimes at the cost of great effort and expense to undo what someone else did at the cost of great effort and expense.

To me, as an admitted purist, marshes with man-made dams or ditches do not have quite the undefiled look of marshes having ancient ice ridges or heaps of glacial rock and clay holding the water. They do not look quite as once looked so many of the marshes that I knew in my youth in eastern South Dakota, before so many people coveted the soil of the bottoms. But reverted or restored or artificial marshes still have their values as marshes, along with the naturally impounded ones remaining in the glacial basins. Whether thinking as a purist or not, I am encouraged by the knowledge that conservation of our wetlands and balanced programs for their use are becoming more of a public issue that can result not only in agitation but also in well-conceived action. Minnesota,

for example, a state that is rapidly losing many of its marshes to drainage, has one of the most vigorous campaigns on the part of the public to buy up or otherwise safeguard threatened marshes.

•   •   •

Astrophysical forces are surely working toward another ice age for our earth. I doubt if man, though he master atomic energy, will be able to circumvent the next glaciation and the erasure by glaciation of the outward manifestations of many of his drainage successes and failures. Whatever may then be left of the present forms of marsh life, I think that there will be glacial marshes on earth after man is gone as a species—that is, unless man destroys himself and all earth-bound life. If he continues to gain power without proportional responsibility, he could do exactly that.

2. of marshes and spring

Spring, to marshland life on the north-central prairies, comes any time from midwinter to hot weather.

Sometimes, it comes almost as a prolongation of a winter thaw. I saw migrating Canada geese in a wet eastern South Dakota in early February. I can still remember a small flock that appeared over a low hilltop, their clamor preceding and following them. Another year, a South Dakota spring came somewhat as a continuation of fall, with not enough winter cold to seal over the streams, and, when it should have snowed, it rained. That was not the way winter usually was in the Dakotas of my younger years. It was more usual to have snow when there should be snow and snow when there should be rain.

On the calendar, spring sometimes comes when the snow is as deep and the ice as thick and as hard and the temperature as low as in the severest part of the winter. Twenty below zero Fahrenheit or colder and a two-foot snowfall in April must still be considered winter in actuality. Snow on plum blossoms and June snowdrifts must still be classed as snow. But the tracks of the wide-ranging minks during their late-winter breeding season are laid down in powdery snow or in slush, on wet sand or on frozen mud or on dry soil. Restless skunks emerge from hibernation long before the weather could tell them to, and great horned owls incubate and brood their young right on through late February and March and

April blizzards. As sexual awakening progresses in the muskrat populations living out of sight of human eyes in their lodges and burrow systems, more and more animals come out and sit on the ice on mild days, until, with the ice gone, the main dispersal away from crowded wintering quarters begins.

Spring comes for much aquatic life when surface waters pour over the ice and down underneath through cracks and holes. The floating ice rises, and vortices with foam-caps appear. The air-gulping bullheads of the muskrat channels and the ice ridges swim away, leaving behind them the bodies of those that died. Water insects and crustacea float or are carried by wind or currents over the ice or in the eddies of the vortices, and some of them may move and some may not. Cracks widen, their edges become smooth, and the waters beneath invite small boys to peer and to stir and probe with poles.

As the floating ice melts and evaporates on top, the lower layers become upper layers. The winter-killed fish collect on the surface to soften or to dry, depending upon whether they lie in or out of the water. About this time, the gulls come and, together with the crows that were around all winter, eat on the fish remains and the remains of turtles, snails, crayfishes, young dragonflies, and the other dead creatures a marsh presents to scavengers in spring. If there were heavy winter-killing, windrows of dead bullheads, pike, sunfishes, perch, buffalo, or the introduced carp surround the open spaces, or thousands of their rounded bellies protrude like pale bald heads from the water amid the rush stems. Where the frost sank deep under the mud margins, the frozen layer beneath the surface may detach itself from the unfrozen mud beneath that, with the result that large areas of marsh bottom float exposed; and the gulls and crows work over this exposed mud for animal remains. The frozen mud melts and settles to the bottom again.

Dispersing muskrats travel along marsh and lake edge, along streams and up gullies. They may act like cautious and adaptive explorers knowing what they are doing as they do it. They may get started in footloose and hazardous wandering and show up on city streets or in farmyards or in any number of out-of-the-way places— if they live long enough. They may travel far or they may not. Living uncertainly or living securely, they behave like muskrats. They hide or fight, doing their best to stay alive, somehow.

Salamanders and garter snakes crawl out of large and small holes on the hillsides while ice can be seen within. Let spring come as a series of warm and rainy nights, and tiger salamanders seem to have inherited the earth. For a couple of days thereafter, about everything predatory that is able and disposed to do so kills salamanders, to eat them or not, until the run is over. Dogs sicken from mouthing them, children take them to school, and horned owls gorge.

•   •   •

In spring, I always feel that the marshes belong to the ducks. There may be loons or the big white or gray herring gulls, flocks of pelicans or cormorants, or herons, grebes, coots, rails, terns, shore birds, swallows, blackbirds, and muskrats all over the place. There may be the mass song of toads and frogs, or countless turtles, or the wakes of fishes. Sometimes there is something special to see, such as whistling swans putting on a courtship display, or flights of calling geese passing overhead or their flocks resting on the water, or an eagle in a dead tree or an osprey in the air. But there must be ducks, too. A north-central marsh without ducks in the spring would not be the full equivalent of a spring without life, but it would be lacking in what belongs.

The spectacles afforded by the ducks in spring vary from year to· year, from week to week, and even—but usually to a less pronounced extent at the height of migration—from day to day.

At first, a few flocks of mallards or pintails may be seen far overhead, or the birds may be alighting on the ice, next to patches of open water that are no more than big puddles on the surface. They sit around hunched or stand with heads up, looking twice as large as they are.

Instead of a few flocks in the air, the spring flight of the mallards and pintails may attain massive proportions like a great wave. I was working out on the still-safe ice of a northern Iowa marsh when the fore part of such a migratory wave appeared in the sky—mostly in large, wary flocks. In another half hour, a fog—allowing about twenty yards of visibility—settled over the marsh. I became aware of ducks by the thousands and thousands, flying all over and around me. As I moved, they veered a little, their bodies and the sounds of their calls and wing beats becoming of the fog again. When I stood still, trying to make out the landmarks of familiar muskrat lodges and rush and reed clumps, they hovered and dropped down. They sat and swam, and more came to hover or drop or pass by. The mallards and pintails were barely out of reach and their colors bright, or, farther away, their dim bodies faded into invisibility. Then, as late-afternoon fatigue warned me not to be caught by darkness wandering over more than a square mile of marsh, I headed for shore, and the ducks made way to let me pass.

Soon, the ice may start melting through in the vicinity of cracks or muskrat channels or spring holes or heating vegetation beneath, or at the places last to freeze over. Wind-blown surface waters nibble at the edges of the ice about these openings, and needles separate and fall into the water and drift against the next shelf of needles ready for falling. Wavelets become waves as the openings enlarge.

American or red-breasted mergansers appear in the spreading open patches, along with goldeneyes and the first flocks of ringnecks and bluebills. Buffleheads sit or dive pertly or engage in flurries of fights. The formal blacks and whites dominate the color patterns of spring dress, but greens and purples also stand out, and there are blends as well as contrasts. The diving ducks fly in pairs or small flocks from one open patch to another.

After a day or two of warm weather and strong winds, the ice may be ready to break up completely. More ringnecks and bluebills come, and among them may be canvasbacks. There may be groups of plain coots among the ducks. Many flocks of mallards are in the air, close by or flying high. There may be a few pairs or small flocks of green-winged teal, shovelers, baldpates.

Another warm, windy day may take out the ice, leaving the remnant of the melting needles in windrows along shore, together with drifting vegetation. Or, that last warm, windy day may not come just then; the weather is wintry again, and the open water seals except for the patches crowded with the ducks and coots.

As the snow blows over the frozen slush and the new ice thickens, crows start picking at dead coots. Other coots flutter where the spray froze, their wings or feathers caught. Still other coots walk on the adjoining land, looking for green grass under the snow. After a couple of days more, they start dying everywhere on the marsh. Minks drag the thin carcasses into holes, and foxes and skunks work the shores.

The ducks get along better than the coots during spring cold snaps. Mallards feed in the cornfields and rest on the ice or swim in the open places, and so do some of the pintails. Perhaps half of the diving ducks leave, and the others dive and usually get enough to eat so that they do not starve. The mergansers and goldeneyes, if they found fish or insect life to attract them to the first open waters, are likely to stay on. The peculiar whistle of goldeneye wings carries over the marsh as the birds search for more open water to drop into.

The weather changes once more, and soon the ice is gone. The ducks and geese reappear in mass movements. In a day's time, the marsh is covered and the air is full of them. Spring is truly spring.

Human responsiveness to the sights and sounds of great numbers of these birds moving northward must be due to more than relief that winter is over, or to anything one might call romantic appeal, or to mere symbolism. It is so very natural for people to respond to the calls in the night and to the life in the skies that this responsiveness must have evolved with mankind—or at least with the northern races—since man's earlier times. Alice Nordin's statues of Danish children watching wild geese portray something basic in many of us, something identifiable in part with love of what is living and free.

I had a small boy with me one windy spring day while walking an Iowa lake shore. As we neared a slough that was separated from the lake by an ice ridge, I thought that there might be something to see, so we crawled up to the ridge and slowly raised our heads. Virtually all of the ducks that had been using the lake were on the slough, in the shelter of the ridge. We had not intended to disturb them, but those near us started getting up and flying over our heads into the wind. As they got up, their neighbors did, and the other neighboring ducks in their turn, until the whole mass arose, all flying only a few yards high and so slowly that we could watch individual ducks for a perceptible interval of time. I pointed out to the boy examples of a dozen species as the strung-out flight continued and then noted such delight on his face that I could hardly look at the ducks again until they were out over the lake.

•　　•　　•

Although each spring's flight of ducks in the north-central region retains the typical components—like the mallards and pintails coming early and the blue-winged teal and shovelers coming later—some years may practically be called diving duck years. Then, thousands of ringnecks or bluebills gather on marshes that had only hundreds the year before and may have only hundreds the year following. They may cover the deeper waters of a lake or marsh at times, and, when feeding, their dark and white bodies disappear under water and pop up again wherever one looks. Along with the thousands of ringnecks and bluebills may be hundreds of the comparatively scarce redheads and canvasbacks, sometimes in places where they have not been seen for several years.

The annual differences in composition of flights do not primarily reflect annual differences in general abundance of duck species. However much may be due to chance, weather, food and water conditions, flock leadership, or to something else, some groups of birds go up one river valley or chain of lakes and marshes and other groups go elsewhere. Neither individuals nor flocks are bound to do it exactly the same way each year.

As spring advances, the mallards and pintails sit in pasture ponds, in plowed-field puddles, about marsh edges, and in the centers of lakes. Blue-winged teal, shovelers, and baldpates predominate in the shallows. Bluebills hang around until it would seem that they might never reach their arctic and subarctic breeding grounds in time to nest, but, about the time when spring comes in the Far North, they disappear almost suddenly—except for the sick and the crippled swimming high in the water, moping on the muskrat lodges, and dying along the shores.

The ducks of mid-spring are mainly in pairs and in threes—two males attending a female—even when associated as flocks, but remarkable exceptions may be observed as the last unmated females attract convoys of surplus males. Baldpate males seem to have a special propensity for trooping after lone females. If a flock of these white-topped males flies erratically over the marsh, one may guess that somewhere among them is a female, though she may not always be distinguishable among the wheeling, dipping bodies. Where she goes, they go, up or down or to the side. When she alights, they alight; when she gets up, they get up. I recall a female baldpate, with about twenty males following, flying across Little Wall Lake. Before she got much of a start, a smaller group of males, without a female of their own to follow, attached themselves to her retinue, and away they all went, until nearing the other side. Then, the newcomers split away from the original group. The others kept going, flying up, flying down, to right and to left for as far as I could see.

Fighting among the buffleheads is so characteristic as to be recognizable even if one can not see the birds themselves. Out on a lake covered with ducks and on which hardly a duck in hundreds is a bufflehead, a certain type of rapid splashing here and there in a small area signifies fighting buffleheads. At a distance, one may be reminded of ricocheting bullets or of water droplets on a hot surface or of something else other than buffleheads, but, out there, they still remind one of buffleheads, too—buffleheads behaving as one comes to expect them to behave. If someone tries to get the splashy areas within the field of binocular or telescope, the buffleheads may be gone—nothing in sight but the ringnecks and pintails and mallards and the other common ducks. Then, a little black and white may show on the surface and disappear and, off to the side, some more black and white may appear and disappear, mostly to stay under the surface as long as diving is the thing to do. Another name for the bufflehead is spirit duck.

The fighting, spiriting buffleheads left one of their number behind them on a marsh to which I made frequent visits. When I saw this solitary drake remaining in central Iowa long past its proper time, I assumed that it was lead poisoned. However, when flushed, it seemed to have only a muscle or a joint injury—presumably the wages of recklessness in making fighting passes at other drake buffleheads. On each occasion that I paddled a canoe past its favorite sitting place, it flew with increasing strength. From a beating flight of twenty yards barely off the water, its flights lengthened to fifty to eighty yards in about a month. I last saw it in early June, as it raised in front of the canoe to fly about a half mile, to alight at the far end of the marsh. I suppose that, soon thereafter, it headed for the lands and waters of buffleheads in summer.

The watcher on a north-central glacial marsh gets many other memorable sights of ducks in spring. Ruddy duck males always astonish people who see them in breeding plumage for the first time. The chunkiness of their bodies and necks, their short, stiff tail feathers held in upright fans, and their cocky bearing are enough to attract attention. A close view of the blue-colored bill and the white cheek patch reminds one so much of ornamental porcelain thickly daubed with paint that it seems strange that anything having such a made-up look could be real and natural and alive—and then the painted porcelain decides that the observer is too close, and dives. It may or may not reappear in sight on the surface. It usually does not have to be seen if it does not want to, if the water is wind-roughened or if there is floating or emergent vegetation to hide a bill stuck out for air.

Canvasbacks look big and are big. Their large breast muscles in combination with rather small wings give capabilities of great and sustained speed when in full flight, but their take-off from the water looks like hard work, and a slightly hunched appearance of the bodies in gaining momentum in the air looks like more hard work. Under water, they are highly expert, and, like the ruddies, can do about what they want to. Whatever they do, healthy, un-injured, grown canvasbacks are an embodiment of power, and of beauty, with streamlined heads and bills, with the contrasts of black, white, and red in the males and the modest blends in the females.

Redheads are, in their way, as distinctive as their close relatives the canvasbacks, and it is as much of an event to see them on our north-central marshes. Both redheads and canvasbacks have de-clined in recent decades, and many of those we do see now are victims of that curse of shot-over waters, lead poisoning.

All species of ducks are beautiful in spring, I think, perhaps in part simply because they are ducks. The shoveler has what might be considered an ugly bill, but it looks all right to me; it belongs on a shoveler. Whatever may be the patterns and extremes of coloration of the ducks, from the drabness of females to the ir-idescent greens and purples and the near-gaudiness of some of the males, they are of living colors. The long-necked pintail male has a white "shirt-front" contrasting with its brown head. The wild mallard is no more beautifully colored than many of the barnyard ducks descended from it, but there is a *difference*; as one sees wild mallards arising out of the bulrushes in front of a canoe, one can see that these are real ducks. So are the black ducks real ducks, and their dusky plumages belong on *them*. And so are the little green-winged teal real ducks, and so are all that truly belong on our marshes, of species that have been there since before the white man came.

· · ·

A feeling that north-central marshes belong to the ducks in spring should not preclude enjoyment of the other native species that belong there, too.

To some people, the white pelicans give the impression of stateliness; to others, of awkwardness. To me, the pelicans, stately or awkward, or both, are magnificent birds and they remind me of the South Dakota prairies of my youth, where they could be seen at almost any time between spring and fall. There is nothing really like their ponderous flapping and sailing in full flight as a long line circles over the water or disappears in the distance, or their dipping of big bills as they fish, or the kicks of their orange-colored legs as they take wing.

Those rather distant and very different relatives of the pelicans, the cormorants, with goose-like flight in air and loon-like skill under water, are seen now and then on many north-central lakes and marshes in spring. Where they have nesting colonies, they are prominent among the bird life. They are hated by some fishermen, but often because of misunderstanding. One of the biggest problems in fisheries management in fertile inland waters is stunting of fish populations through overcrowding, and, when this is what is wrong, any feeding by fish-eating wildlife that eliminates large quantities of stunted fishes (including game or pan fishes) works for the betterment of the fishing.

Of other diving birds, I always enjoy watching the loons and the elongated western grebes, neither of which are often seen passing through central Iowa. The cormorants, loons, and grebes are capable of submerging until only their heads and necks are out, or partly out, of the water, or until only bill tips are out—or until nothing is in sight. They may be appearing and disappearing all over a body of water, or just sitting on a quiet surface or riding waves. The commonest on most north-central waters are the small pied-billed grebes, but, along with pied bills, we occasionally see a few that are still smaller, the eared grebes, with their pointed bills and black and buff crests.

Great blue herons may be seen standing in the deeper shallows of the shore zone or wherever they find shallows, or on the feeding platforms of muskrats or on matted vegetation in deep-water marsh. Their flight is ungainly yet has its grace. One watching it can imagine himself watching the flying reptiles of a younger earth. Thick stands of sedges or bulrushes may be taken over by black-crowned night herons, and we may see the whites of their heads sticking out of the tops of medium-height vegetation, or they may stand around the marsh or lake edges or cluster in trees or fly heavily (but well enough) about the edges or across the water. They tend more to congregate than do the other of our north-central herons.

Green herons, made up chiefly of necks, frequent the willow fringes and wet edges, and, when in sight, are usually in the trees or flying away along the shore. American bitterns belong more to the rushy or weedy or slightly open marsh edges or the boggy places. The least bitterns, of blackbird size but genuine bitterns with the form and flight and posture of their larger relatives, are birds of the bulrush and cattail stands of the marsh depths, though some may be flushed from the weedy growths of the shore.

The herons are the patient birds. So much of their life is spent just waiting, when hunting as well as digesting. They stalk slowly in the shallows, partly stooped over; then they wait and wait; and, when they stab toward water or mud or into the grass, the movement is often so effortless as to be almost unnoticeable. There may be some manipulation of the prey with the beak or contorting of the neck as the prey is swallowed, then the waiting again. The prey may be easily swallowable fishes or formidably spiny bullheads or some things too large to go down all at once. Or prey may be frogs or mice or small snakes, crayfishes or large insects, including water bugs and beetles, dragonflies, and grass-hoppers. Great blue herons sometimes prey on ground-squirrels and pocket gophers.

For some species in some places, the designation "fish-eating bird" is just a name. Except for the osprey, which I have never seen feeding upon anything but fishes, members of fish-eating groups eat a wide variety of animal material. Mergansers (called fish-ducks) of all North American species may stay about a fishless marsh, getting along well on a diet mostly of tadpoles or aquatic insects.

The rails make up another group of marsh birds. The common ones are the soras, though there are other species living about north-central marshes. The soras run over the rafted bulrush debris or swim between the rafts or, when alarmed, lift up into flight to drop down again into the next concealing stand of vegetation. The other rails of like size or smaller—the Virginia and yellow rails— are seldom seen except when their remains are found at feeding places of predators. Sometimes, one may glimpse a bird that looks a little like a young turkey skulking through the thick growths—a king rail. But, however secretive about exposing themselves to sight the rails are, some can be noisy, and their medley of call notes is part of a living marsh.

The American coot, a member of the rail family, can be a conspicuous bird in places having much open water. Coots cover certain waters at certain times, and, as their breeding season advances, the territorial combativeness of the individuals remain-ing to nest is demonstrated not only toward other coots but also toward other waterfowl big enough to draw attack and small enough to be bullied. Blue-winged teal may be driven from certain places by coots, but, if the teal want to stay there, they soon return.

When I was young, the sandhill cranes, large relatives of the rails and coots, were of the north-central prairies. Most Americans who talk of cranes misapply the name to the quite different large herons. Away from the scattered areas in the northern Lake States where a few cranes persist, one has to go westward in our region to see real free-living cranes or to hear their bugling.

• • •

The time comes when a canoe paddle no longer strikes frozen bottom. The ducks are gone except for the stragglers and the ailing and those remaining to nest. Red-winged blackbirds have established their almost-measured territories along the rushy shores; the yellowheads, their territories in the central reed clumps. In between, both blackbird species may live where there is room for them, sometimes one species dominating, sometimes the other, in very similar environment. Nesting terns dive at one's head. The breeding-season calls—of blackbirds, rails, coots, grebes, sparrows, shore birds, and other good advertisers—join together. On some marshes, the bird sounds become a roar, so much so that a listener cannot distinguish individual sounds.

It may be the time, too, of dead turtles. I recall poling a canoe through about a hundred yards of wet mud in order to approach what I first thought was a heavy, orange-yellow branching root with branches broken off close to a thick tap root—a most peculiar object to be seeing in the middle of a drying marsh. The thick tap root turned out to be the sides and body underparts of a snapper a yard long from tip of tail to a head five inches across. It was lying on its back with gas-distended legs, tail, and neck sticking rigidly in the air. I shall not insist that it was anything beauteous by ordinary human standards, but neither did it lack its qualities of majesty. A lot of animal died when it died, and it had enough left of its image of massive formidability to be worth looking at.

At some times in some springs, puffed-out big snappers—or those of all sizes—float about or drift shoreward in impressive numbers. As waves wash them back and forth where they lodge, their appendages become limp, and then the outstretched heads and necks move with each movement of the water, so flaccidly, in going back to the water and marsh bottom again. As the skeletons wash apart, knobby and plate-like bones become covered with sand or muck, to protrude less and less, and finally one sees little of the older turtle bones any more.

With warmer weather, one sees more of live turtles. Away from shore, blunt points of turtle heads stick out of the water. There may be few or many, of snappers or of painted turtles, appearing and disappearing. There may be large shadowy forms moving slowly beneath the surface or green and red bodies with paddling legs. One may not be thinking of turtles at all, then notice that the body of a lead-poisoned diving duck rocks in the water, floats quietly, moves again like a cork showing the nibble of a fish—only it is not a fish that is nibbling. It is a painted turtle, and, as it reaches its head upward to take hold of the duck's neck or wing or leg or whatever else offers it a purchase, we can think or say, if we wish, that its eyes have a cold reptilian stare. The turtle will not mind what we think or say as long as we leave it alone. It has its living to do and it fastens its horny bill, pulls in its neck, and pushes itself away from the duck's body with its forefeet until something comes loose.

And, with summer, the familiar heat and lengthening days. The midges hum, new shoots of rush and reed and cattail appear above the water, waterlilies float their new pads and flowers, masses of arrowheads take form, and newly weaned muskrats swim and sit and feed and dress themselves as if they thought they amounted to something. In dry weather, the high-water stains on the old dead plant stems extend farther and farther above the surface, or rain waters may refill the marsh, with the regularity and irregularity of past ages. Life remains there, adjusting, living when and where and how and if it can.

3. *of marshes and summer*

To know what summer really can be on a north-central glacial marsh, one must go either westward or northward from Iowa—or, better, northwestward into northeastern South Dakota. A century ago, Iowa's marshes may have been like those to the west, north, or northwest. Old paintings of pre-settlement Iowa prairies have lark buntings perched on the horns of bison skulls, big shore birds distributed over the landscape, and other types of life that we now seldom find before we leave the state.

The marshes of northwest Iowa resemble most closely those of the South Dakota of my youth, but little that I have ever seen in Iowa compares with what was once commonplace a few hundred miles away. Iowa's marshes do have eastern and southern features that my old South Dakota marshes lacked. I never saw in South Dakota the white American egrets standing around in late summer, nor the wood ducks summering by the hundreds in the reedy and rushy marsh centers, nor the thousands of least bitterns that I have seen in Iowa. It is also on Iowa rather than on South Dakota sloughs that I have seen non-breeding hooded mergansers spending the breeding months and colonies of night herons nesting in the marsh itself instead of in the trees.

Some of these differences over the north-central region may but reflect an observer's opportunities or the local changes in distribution of this or that species over the years. In other cases, the nature of the plant and animal life and the adjustments of living things to special kinds of environment bring change. Populations may be expected to thin out as their requisites become scarce toward the edges of their range. No species thrives where it does not belong.

There are also the teasing questions of environmental niches and competition between closely related species. The black duck is the mallard's counterpart over much of eastern North America, and, where the ranges of the two overlap in the north-central region, we generally find one thriving much more than the other. To the west, we have the breeding range of the blue-winged teal merging with that of its western counterpart, the cinnamon teal, with places in their common range where the proportions of nesting blue-winged and cinnamon teal are highly variable.

Among the other factors that may determine what lives where and when are droughts that force adjustments in ranges, but not all adjustments are so patently forced. Increasing populations of migratory birds may return to a given locality to breed after special nesting traditions have been established. Or, tracts of otherwise suitable habitat may long remain unfilled, if the birds lose their traditions for nesting there.

Certain differences are nevertheless characteristic of different parts of our region, and these may be maintained over periods of years, irrespective of ordinary annual variations in marsh life. Perhaps the marshes of northeastern South Dakota have so noticeably greater a variety of marsh birds than do central and northern Iowa marshes largely because of their location deep in extensive marshland areas. On a marsh-by-marsh basis, northeastern South Dakota would not seem to offer perceptibly better environment to, let us say, nesting pintails than places that offer similar water, vegetation, and terrain in Iowa; but, to the pintails, Iowa is edge-of-range, and northeastern South Dakota is in the midst of favored nesting grounds.

•　　　•　　　•

No one view could typify a marsh of eastern South Dakota at its life-rich summer best. One view should be of a misty morning with sunlight filtering through, and avocets, willets, and lesser shore birds running along a mud flat, feeding, raising their wings (the willets showing their white bars), and calling. On mud- or sand-bars or floating posts or muskrat lodges, the terns guard their terri-

tories. Over all, the medley of blackbird and bobolink calls, of coot and rail and grebe calls, the pumping of bitterns. In the right places, the booming of prairie chickens is a part of the morning sounds of early summer.

Ducks are much in the marsh picture. Territory-holders sit along shore or on prominences out in the marsh, sometimes both members of the pair, sometimes the males alone. Here they are, nesting in the Dakotas, many of the ducks that were spring migrants through Iowa. On shore are the mallards and pintails, the bald-pates, shovelers, gadwalls, green-winged teal, and especially the blue-winged teal—bluewings everywhere, the males with white crescents on the sides of their heads. Deeper in the marsh are mallards and some other puddle ducks sitting on muskrat lodges. The divers are there, too. They swim or loaf amid the bulrush islands or sit in the open. There are the contrasting colors of the male

of marshes and summer   23

divers, the redheads and canvasbacks looking as striking as during migration, the ruddies as artificially painted.

The actual nesting sites of the ducks vary greatly. Most puddle ducks place their nests not in the marsh but in surrounding vegetation, in suitable growths of sedge or cordgrass, or on pastured hillsides or in hayfields. The adaptable mallards nest on tops of haystacks, along the marsh edges, and out in the marsh on muskrat lodges. Pintails may nest on the uplands a couple of miles away from a marsh, then lead their broods overland to the water. The real diving ducks usually build their nests in rush clumps, though ringnecks may put them on muskrat lodges or near water's edge along shore.

Many ducks, in addition to their normal nesting, lay eggs in the nests of other species of ducks. All of our ducks probably do this to some extent (as well as laying in nests of like-sized birds other than ducks), but the redheads and ruddies engage in such "parasitism" almost habitually. I am not sure how well this works out for the "parasitizing" species, though an odd duckling may be seen, apparently getting along, in the brood of another species. Of course, it does not always follow that the odd duckling hatched with the others, for, after hatching, considerable splitting up and recombination of broods may take place, this becoming more and more conspicuous late in the rearing season.

·   ·   ·

By midsummer, the greenery of the sedges, bulrushes, cattails, and reeds conceals much of the animal life of a marsh, but, when there is so much life that the marsh seems almost to boil over, one is not likely to think about what remains hidden. Up ahead in an open space, one sees a brood of bluewings (or of almost any other duck that rears young there) swimming or flapping for the shelter of the rushes as one approaches in a canoe. A brood of ruddies may submerge with their mother, or a few tiny pied-bill grebe chicks may leave a hatching clutch of eggs to dive and come up a few feet away—or perhaps become entangled in submerged vegetation. There are young terns, swimming with bodies low in the water, while adults frantically hover over them and swoop at intruders. There are weaned young muskrats that sit, eat, and swim about a lodge or rush raft. Heavy-ended fledgling blackbirds attempt their first flights from one reed clump to another, losing altitude as they fly, and finally they clamber among the canes by means of their strong feet.

Low over the marsh, the self-hunting young marsh hawks quarter back and forth, dipping down and rising up to make passes at other young creatures. These hawks in their buffy juvenile plumage can be so monotonously unsuccessful in their attacks that one wonders how they stay alive long enough to learn to hunt. They make out with what they mooch from the older hawks, or with what they find dead, or with the unwary or sluggish or weak mammals and birds that fall victim now and then, or with the grasshoppers and crickets and small snakes that they catch away from the marsh itself. Even so, amid an abundance of prospective prey, they work for a living.

In my notes of years ago is an account of a young marsh hawk taken in as the lone survivor from a mowed-over nest. After a month and a half of rearing on a diet of ground-squirrels and black-birds, it was, in early August, given a stuffing of blackbird meat and released, banded, near a marsh-edge shack. Six days later, I saw a young marsh hawk hunting over a meadow a half mile from the shack. The bird came near and alighted in a tree, its band showing plainly. It was hungry and wanted something done. I ran back to the shack for a gun, shot a few blackbirds, and then ran with the blackbirds back to the marsh hawk. When I was within about sixty yards of the hawk—which was sitting where I left it—it flew toward me, and I threw it a blackbird, which it carried off to the meadow to eat. The next day, I went looking for my hawk and found it still in the neighborhood; it came up to me, caught the blackbird I tossed in the air, and away it went once more.

For hawks that get plenty to eat, the moisture content of their food may suffice in the hottest of midwest weather, but the long fasts of self-hunting young necessitate a certain amount of drinking. One hot day, I sat down to rest in the shade of a willow beside the water, and, the next I knew, a young marsh hawk was standing in the shallows close to me and drinking like a farmyard chicken from a dish. It gave such an impression of looking everywhere at once that I dared not move more than eyelids. I felt mosquitoes on my neck and face but let them bite, until the hawk, after a time, flew to a shaded dead tree.

Through "reading sign," we learn of the animal life in the dense vegetation of the shallow shore zones. It is true that blackbirds and sparrows and wrens fly about, that we may flush a rail or an American bittern or perhaps surprise a raccoon or a skunk along shore, but the trails and feeding places tell much more of what goes on.

Trails run in shallow water, between or under the heavy growths, with muskrat cuttings in little piles to the side, and some of these trails extend into the shore growths. A trail is a trail for any kind of creature that wants to use a trail. It is followed by everything from mice and frogs up to the larger mammals. Shore trails serve as main highways of travel or branch into networks of lesser trails. They tend to be favored by predators that eat crayfishes.

The mink trails are the ones that I like to study, for they reflect so much of the day-by-day drama of the marsh edge. Either in the trails or at the openings of den sites—such as holes in the upper parts of old muskrat burrows—the "sign" tells of staple diets of crayfishes and frogs, or of water beetles or dragonflies or blackbirds or young coots. The mink trails are sometimes littered with clam shells where the marsh is lake-like, or with dry land prey when the minks have access to an inviting source of mice, ground-squirrels, grasshoppers, or land birds. On duck marshes, there may be ducks of all ages in the mink trails and pulled into the den holes; on muskrat marshes, muskrats may be among the conspicuous victims.

Hunters or trappers may regard these dead ducks or muskrats with something less than pleasure, but it is easy to arrive at wrong answers as to what this predation means in terms of duck and muskrat populations. Mink predation upon muskrats has been studied with particular thoroughness on Iowa marshes and proves to be, under normal conditions, mainly a matter of the minks utilizing part of the biological wastage of muskrat populations. Up to midsummer, nearly all of the muskrats preyed upon by minks on the Iowa areas are the strife-battered excess males that are forced to wander and live in dangerous places because of the intolerance of their better-situated fellow muskrats. In mid- and late summer, most of the mink victims are either surplus young similarly forced into the dangerous shore zones to keep out of the way of their intolerant elders, or animals placed under overwhelming disadvantage through storm or drought emergencies. Mink victims, therefore, are not just any individuals that minks care to prey upon, but rather those falling into special classes of vulnerability before becoming victims.

Muskrat flesh also becomes available to minks in substantial quantities at times of epidemics. Some minks modify their usual habits to take advantage of such sources of food. Instead of living in the crayfish-rich shore zones, they maintain summer residence far out in a marsh in the midst of disease "hotspots" as long as the dying of the muskrats continues.

For two consecutive summers, minks stayed over from spring in deep-marsh "hotspots" on a northern Iowa study area, and, each summer, I came to recognize at least three of the minks individually. The muskrat lodges taken over by the minks had a tousled appearance from surface nests in which the minks slept. I would slip up to these nests in a canoe, hoping to find a mink asleep and sometimes doing so. Then, I would note marking patterns and color differences and perhaps watch the breathing movements of the curled-up, partly-buried body for a few minutes because I liked to. Sometimes, I could withdraw unnoticed by the wild one. Sometimes, it would rear up and face me for an instant before hitting the water with explosive suddenness. Or, the nest might become empty in front of my eyes, the loose vegetation of the top of the lodge might quiver, and there might be a soft splash with a string of bubbles coming up from a straight underwater trail. The mink might surface in plain sight close by, or the bubble trail might disappear in the rushes, and the rush stems move a little and continue moving a little, farther and farther away.

The lodge tops frequented by the minks of the marsh center have their coarse remains—the wings and large bones and skins—of terns, grebes, coots, rails, and blackbirds, as well as of ducks and muskrats. Feather debris extends down into the holes leading to the old muskrat chambers, and, when the outside of a lodge is littered, the inside also may be. Latrines reveal much of the smaller prey that is eaten in entirety: the red down and beaks of coot chicks, the dark and light of grebe chicks, and the fur and bones of marsh-dwelling meadow mice.

It is often plain that old bodies are rotten when minks pull them out of the water and leave them on the muskrat lodges. Ducks, coots, grebes, and muskrats, all fuzzy with water mold and with appendages fallen off, may lie there drying or have freshly eaten parts. Granted that hunting or scavenging out in the marsh center may be hard going for the minks at times, the minks may neglect obvious sources of staple prey, such as crayfishes, to feed upon at least muskrat flesh— rotten or not—as long as it is available.

Despite this selectiveness for muskrat flesh and the motivation that dead muskrats offer minks for staying around a spring or early summer disease "hotspot," the minks may not find more than a minor fraction of the bodies of muskrats dying there.

Abundant raccoons, on the other hand, may be so thorough in their warm-weather searching as to leave scarcely any dead muskrats in a local "hotspot" area. One mid-June day, I cruised a notorious "hotspot" and found only two dead muskrats, both floating some distance from lodges. The lodges themselves had been leveled by raccoons over six acres of disease-swept marsh, and there, asleep on a flattened lodge butt two hundred yards from shore, lay a mother and five third-grown raccoons. As the canoe passed near the butt, the young raccoons lying with their masked faces turned in my direction opened their eyes and closed them again.

Sometimes, young minks are kept in a deep-marsh lodge. They may be blind and helpless, tucked away, the whole litter of them, in the old muskrat chamber; or they may flit in and out of holes, not helpless at all. To an observer, there may be intent small faces in the shadow of the holes, withdrawing and coming back again; or there may be no minklets in sight, but from the interior of a lodge may come the grating sounds of quarreling.

As a mink-riddled lodge reeks of marsh dead and blue-bottles fly into and fly out of holes, there may be no more remains appearing, and a neighboring lodge may show mink holes and fresh droppings and some feathers and muskrat fur. Sometimes, minks live in nests or in the lodges long past the time of their feeding upon muskrats. Sometimes, they move to and live in another part of a deep-water marsh having a thriving muskrat population, yet the remains of food in the nests and latrines of the new place have nothing of muskrat. Or later, when the muskrats of the more central parts stop dying, our deep-marsh minks—and raccoons—may go back to shore. That is where the majority of our north-central minks and raccoons spend their summers, anyway.

The marsh edge can be a truly attractive place for predators or scavengers seeking the exploitable. Ailing or overflow animals from the marsh center congregate there, fresh carrion washes in, land forms come to feed or drink or roost. There may be a heron rookery in adjacent trees, with fishes and young herons falling out of the nests. One species may come there to escape enemies, another to find prey. In northern wildernesses, the marsh-edge visitors include wolves, bears, otters, skunks, and minks; in the western high plains, coyotes, badgers, skunks, and minks; in the north-central states, foxes, weasels, raccoons, skunks, and minks. Over most of the continent where glacial marshes occur, the marsh edge may be said to belong to the minks as much as to any single form.

•   •   •

Late summer on a north-central marsh is ordinarily a season of dry, hot weather. Some degree of drought is normal at this time of year over vast continental regions, and the native plant life is adjusted to it. Partial exposure of the bottom promotes the germination of the seeds of important marsh plants—this is one reason why we so often see pothole after pothole with open-water centers and dense fringing growths of cattails and bulrushes. It is when we get extreme drought that the big changes occur.

I have spent much time out in the drying centers of marshes, panting and straining in boot-sucking mud or trying to stay up by walking on waterlily rootstocks. The last inch or two of water on top of the mud may seethe with movements of gills and mouths and backs and tails. Garter snakes swim partly immersed through minnow-filled water or rest on the exposed mud. I have seen big bullheads concentrated by the ton over an acre of mud bottom—hanging on to their lives for many weeks after the last of the other fishes became skeletonized. Or, there may be no fishes left alive. The puddles may be full, instead, of snails, crustaceans, or insect larvae, to be worked over by wading birds or by whatever else there is to take advantage of them.

A little more exposure, and motion ceases over the surface mud. Some creatures go beneath, some become part of a gelatinous film, some persist as shells or bony heads and tails; and these, too, are exploited. The shore birds probe, the creatures of carrion appear. Soft mud hardens and cracks and takes footprints of the heavier animals of the shore zones. The skeletons of the big fishes—perhaps of pike or buffalo—already lie weathering and in process of reclamation by the marsh bottom. Here is the down of a duckling or the woolly fur spread out from the bones of a young muskrat or perhaps a freshly dead young muskrat with belly slashed by an older one. Or something with the dry and shrinking skin of death still moves with life as black and red carrion beetles work beneath.

The snapping turtles leave their double trails of footprints and their drag marks of body and tail—big and little snappers and the in-between sizes, crisscrossing the muddy bottom or following musk-rat paths or the channels of old water currents. They may labor along, their backs heaped with the mud that came up with them as they dug themselves out of a burial spot. There may be as much mud as turtle moving over the bottom, and the muddy heap moves and rests and moves again, or it sinks into the softer mud of a wet spot. There may be a slightly raised spot that moves at intervals out in the soft mud, and then the surface levels off. The snapper is where it belongs, with muddy fish skin and bones, water insects or crayfishes, or a wad of vegetation in stomach or intestine.

Despite racial testing in the muds of millions of droughts, the snapping turtle is not always secure during a drought even if it has mud for refuge. It is not unusual for members of the dog family to locate by smell and dig out a snapper. The snapper might be a little one that a big dog could crush with a bite, or it might be a big one. I remember a place where a family of red foxes dug out and ate a snapper big and formidable enough to have eaten one of them if it had gotten a hold. Judging from the crater in the fox-trampled mud, the hollowed-out turtle shell, and the skinned appendages, the snapper was alive and possessed of its defensive powers at the time of attack. It was likewise apparent that the foxes knew what they were doing, kept away from the snapping end of the turtle, and first ate into the body from behind. The drama of the marsh bottom must have been lively while it lasted, with the foxes taking plenty of sporting chances in attacking such dangerous prey at all.

A series of wet years may be accompanied by either sudden or gradual loss of the emergent vegetation of marshes, and some of the changes brought about thereby are as drastic in their way as the changes of droughts. When a marsh turns into an open-water lake in one season, the evicted marsh-dwellers that cannot fly away may crowd the shores and adjacent land. Muskrats, being among the sufferers from such natural cataclysms, are preyed upon by the usual hunters of shore zones. The vulnerable muskrats, while they last, live in cavities under tree roots, in badger and woodchuck holes, in tile openings and culverts, under piles of junk and in nests fashioned out of drift; they eat what they find close by and raid the corn and beans and small grain of cultivated lands; they appear in grain shocks and farmyards; and they leave their remains wherever they go until their surviving numbers are more in balance with their possibilities for living.

Late summer may bring local algal mats so dense that they smother all plant growths beneath them, so tough and clinging that one cannot paddle a canoe through them. These mats are crossed by surface trails of turtles, birds, and muskrats, just as an exposed bottom could be. The minks come out and hunt the algal trails, littering them with prey debris as they do the marsh-edge trails Where the algal mats and mud are firm enough for walking, the real land mammals of the marsh edge—the skunks and foxes and coyotes —work out farther away from shore, preying and scavenging according to their tastes and opportunities. Sometimes, the algal growths take the form of scums or discolored water, sometimes they are of paint-like coloration, sometimes they mix with those smallest of flowering plants, the duckweeds and water meal.

Marshes may be scenes of mortality for many creatures when algal growths are of poisonous types or when the bacteria responsible for botulism thrive in the stagnant water and decaying organic matter. However, I have seldom witnessed this type of deadliness and then only in certain places. More often, the late summer dying of animal life is apt to involve fishes, whether they die from maturity, oxygen depletion, disease, poisoning, or wholly unknown causes. Or, the dead things may be mainly frogs with reddened legs or snails floating amid discolored duckweeds.

Late summer on the north-central prairies is also a season of spectacular abundance of many species. The flights and roosting of red-winged and yellow-headed blackbirds may be noted by people who never go near marshes. I have seen up to three-quarters of a million red-winged blackbirds—estimated from numbers counted on square-yard samples—roosting after sunset in a single part of a large cattail marsh. Sitting swallows can make telephone wires look like ragged cables in the distance. Along in August, we have the early congregations of ducks. The young blue-winged teal that have not much more than learned to fly gather by hundreds or thousands about the major marshes before embarking on their real southward migration.

The bluewings feed on the pondweed seeds, in singles, in small groups, and in rafts. In their innocence, they may permit an observer to approach within fifteen or twenty yards, then they arise to drop down a hundred yards away, or even wheel and return if they especially liked the feeding bed. Here and there may swim a family of late-hatched ruddies. The warier mallards and pintails may sit farther out, raising heads if anything moves on shore.

of marshes and summer   *31*

Turtles sit on floating logs or stick heads out of the water. A big snapper may cover the top of a small muskrat lodge. Painted turtles may sun themselves in such numbers that they make muskrat lodges look from a distance as if armored by great plates of mail. Garter snakes may line the marsh edge, feeding upon small frogs and being fed upon in their turn by the snake-eaters.

The nights of late summer on or about a marsh are as fascinating in their way as the daytimes, particularly if brightly moon-lit. The word "magic" has been applied to moonlight so nearly generally and for so long that it has become hackneyed, yet such a variety of animal life—including human—responds to moonlight that we need a word that is special and superlative to express our meaning. Combinations of moonlight and mist and shadow effects may promote illusions of enchantment for almost any receptive person. In late summer, the abundance of life is there in the moon-light, too, some of it subdued and hidden and some of it more active than in the daylight. We hear the hissing calls of hungry young horned owls, insisting that their parents continue to feed them long after those parents have lost interest.

A mother mink may be followed by one or two young as she bounds or swims along shore—the last of the litter staying with her after the quarrels of the other young culminated in their going their own way by themselves, as is the way of minks. Somewhere else along the marsh edge, one might glimpse one of these newly self-hunting minks, finding its own crayfishes, eating grasshoppers and garter snakes, noisily running through the vegetation, and perhaps meeting one of its litter mates, perhaps to withdraw, per-haps to fight. Twice, during my years of study of the food habits of minks, I found evidence of partly grown young minks feeding on bodies of other young minks.

• • •

Late summer is a time of pleasant incongruities, as animal life appears outside of accustomed ranges: an ibis or a little blue heron on a northern Iowa marsh, western shorebirds drifting eastward, or what has become by now a fairly regular northward movement of American egrets. One of the strangest out-of-place sights in my memory was of a flock of turkey vultures circling over a Pre-cambrian lake shore in eastern Manitoba. In some cases, the actual extensions of ranges have been so pronounced in late years that it is often difficult to judge what may be a stray and what may be a successful pioneer. It is no longer wholly surprising to see raccoon and timber wolf tracks on the same marsh border if we go far enough—but not too far—north.

• • •

The first faint hints of fall, for me, come with the reappearance on Iowa marsh and lake shores of many species of shore birds that do not remain to breed in the state. It almost seems as if their southward migration begins before the northward migration of the dawdling bluebills has finished. Then, the flights of Franklin's gulls tell that summer is turning into fall, and their wavy lines across the horizon reawaken my memories of virgin Dakota prairies.

I think again of unplowed hills and lowlands covered with native grasses and blazing stars and prairie clovers and vetches and sunflowers and asters and compass plants and cone flowers. I think of withering arrowhead leaves over the waters, of muskrats building lodges, of flocks of pelicans and cormorants along with the gull flocks, of the massed flights of blackbirds, shore birds, and ducks. Always, I think of the ducks, the divers and dabblers, in flight or, in their seasonal tameness, sitting on shore and water. I may think of something commonplace like young jackrabbits or a skunk dropping made up of grasshopper remains. I like to remember the times when I walked in the hills or looked over the water in evenings after the farm chores were done, even after long days of making hay or pitching bundles.

My memory-pictures of the "old days," when summer transformed into fall, are of countrysides having greater natural riches than those I now find close to home. Admittedly, I have my thoughts about values that we collectively let slip, hardly knowing what they were, thoughts about the world of my familiarity being better when there were fewer people and less money, when we did without modern gadgets and were not so impelled to use every acre up to its maximum economic productivity.

The passage of the seasons, however, is still with us as a phenomenon, and there are still marshes and the life of marshes. There are still countrysides having values to be enjoyed and values worth preserving.

4. *of marshes and fall*

As late summer grades off into weeks of autumnal mellowness, the waterfowl migration has the appearance of a leisurely procedure. Puddle ducks cover the shallows and mud flats of the more favored marshes with thousands of loafing, sleeping, feeding bodies. In fall plumage, they look much alike from a distance, except for the long necks of the pintail drakes and the size differences of big ducks and small ducks. When diving ducks are mixed with puddle ducks, the ducks of a general brownish or grayish coloration can be hard to identify. I have often thought that I must be looking at something new or special, only to have the bird in question finally resolve itself into an ordinary green-winged teal or ringneck or pintail hen. Here and there are birds in the midst of plumage changes, with green or black or other mottlings, or, rarely, there may be a hybrid that does not fit anywhere.

Among the diving ducks, ruddies may occupy almost every pond or slough having water deep enough for them to dive in. Usually, there are ringnecks present this early in the season, along with some redheads and canvasbacks and occasionally a few white-winged scoters that seem almost as large as geese. The divers may include many bluebills or goldeneyes, their numbers varying with geography, even within a particular region.

Away off by themselves, a flock of Canada geese or mixed blues and snows may sit along the edge of a slough in some big flat pasture, extremely wary of anyone's approach on foot, yet sometimes flying directly overhead. As they fly in flock formation, their separate family groupings are still maintained. Their big bodies and slow wing beats make them seem to fly slowly, but when they sweep by, close over one's head, the illusion of slowness is lost.

The waterfowl migration before heavy frosts may not be as quiescent as it seems. There is evidence of movement in the appearance and disappearance of rarities that stand out in the general assemblages—a cinnamon teal or an old squaw duck or something else that we do not often see on Iowa or Dakota marshes. (One mild, early-fall day in South Dakota, I crouched within five yards of a European widgeon.) Or there may be noticeable changes in numbers of ducks, as when a marsh gains, overnight, several hundreds of baldpates, then, after a day or two, they are gone. Mallards outnumber the pintails for a time, or the pintails outnumber the mallards. There may be a local build-up of wood ducks until they outnumber some species we usually think of as far more commonplace on glacial marshes.

Grebes live in the sloughs with the ruddy ducks, still more reluctant than the ruddies to fly as long as they can dive. Food-rich waters are black with coots. Beaches have their shore birds of differing sizes and shapes and colors, running, wheeling in flight, standing, calling, probing. There might be dowitchers flying in a compact flock or working the mud with long bills; jacksnipes flushing in swift, erratic flight or flying high over the marsh; occasional big godwits and curlews, showing up conspicuously among the yellowlegs and sandpipers and killdeers; perhaps, some turnstones or stocky black-bellied plovers. I remember a distant view of what I first thought was a flock of a dozen and a half ducks, but soon knew that they were not ducks and recognized them as big shore birds. Later in the day, I saw that they were willets. They passed over me as I pushed a canoe among the central rush clumps of the marsh, and they circled and passed over me several times more, uttering the wildest of gull-like cries.

Chronically ravenous young marsh hawks hunt over marsh edges and surrounding lands and open fields. Kingfishers sit at lookout perches and fly rattling along shore. There are the crows. There are the migrating sharp-shinned and pigeon hawks from the northern forests—mostly youngsters, acting as hungry as the young marsh hawks. There are the swallows, and, on the right day at the right place, a person may sit or lie on a windy hilltop and have bank swallows flying all around. They fly against the wind, to the edge of an updraft, hover, sweep away, and beat their way back, low over the ground, again and again. At a distance, a large flock of blackbirds looks like dust; the flock turns one way, and the individual specks blacken and become distinct; it turns another way, and the whole flock disappears from view, as quickly as the closing of a shutter. Or the air over a marsh may be so full of flying blackbirds that one has trouble distinguishing other birds while the flight continues, or the blackbirds may alight in the emergent vegetation in such numbers that they weigh it down.

By mid-September to early October, most of the big and little herons may be gone, but marsh edges still have their American bitterns. The bitterns fly out of the vegetation at one's approach or they face one with head and neck pointed upward, trying to look like something else. In their approximation of invisibility through position and markings they blend into their background of vegetation, but, to me, their eyes are often a give-away. The body could be a stick or part of a cattail stalk—then I find myself looking at eyes that are looking at me, an eye on each side of the rigidly held, upward-pointing bill. The expression I read into a bittern's eyes is one of complete distrust.

In the right places, the air and water and land edges have their white pelicans and blackish cormorants and the gulls. As a former Dakotan, I think of the clean colors of the Franklin's gull, of black and white and reddish and slaty markings; of waving flights and circling flights, of flights in great eddies, of swoops and dips, of sweet calls; of glinting wings and bodies far off, of birds sitting on water or covering new plowings or massing where the grasshoppers were thickest in stubble and mowed hayfields. I remember gulls so tame that they alighted and rode on the backs of the plow-horses. They flew about me, just out of reach, like a cloud of big butterflies.

I think of butterflies, too, and woolly-bear caterpillars and many other forms of prairie life in the fall. Skunk families search the glacial hills and marsh edges, and their droppings show the red and yellows and serrations of grasshopper legs. There may be coyotes and jackrabbits, midges and crayfish mounds. Frogs feed on grasshoppers or sit near the water, and, after a time, human eyes see little of them. Salamanders crawl toward their wintering holes. Minks leave their tracks in sand and mud, their droppings and prey remain on rocks, logs, boards, open spaces, and at the entrances of holes.

Sometimes, one sees something amusing. In a pool next to a cornfield, I saw rolling in the water an object that resembled a fur-covered basketball. The basketball spread out into a five-pointed star made up of five muskrats, each with teeth anchored to a nubbin of corn in the center. They tugged and they rolled and they whined, and, when an animal lost its hold on the corn, it would soon get back on. Finally, an enterpriser got the nubbin all to itself and whisked away, leaving the others swimming in circles. But, in a few moments, the others seemed to forget their loss and became their tending-to-own-business selves again.

•   •   •

My memories of marshes in fall are so loaded with nostalgia that I often find myself enjoying Iowa or Minnesota or Nebraska marshes largely to the extent that they remind me of my youth and early manhood in South Dakota. I find old copper bases of shotgun shells working out of an Iowa beach, read the "U.M.C.," "New Rival," "Referee," "Premier," along with other trademarks that long ago disappeared from hardware shelves, and visualize the distinctive colors of the cartridges as they came out of the cardboard boxes. I remember wet shells so swollen that I could not push them into the chamber of a gun, shells that would not always fire if I did get them in, the bellow and smoke of a heavy charge of black powder, the smell of a freshly fired case, the feel of a jolted shoulder, the picking up of game.

As a hunter in the old days, I was not so much a sportsman as I was a predator living off the country. It was by hunting and trapping in combination that I once made a substantial part of my living; and I did so chiefly to be able to spend more time on the marshes. The era of market hunting passed shortly before I started my own hunting, but the open seasons were still long and the bag and possession limits still large, and game remained staple diet on our marsh-side farm for many months at a stretch, as well as at my trapping camps in late fall and winter. Of the game available to us in those years, we liked most of all and naturally had most of all: ducks, ducks, ducks.

My favorite memories of fall marshes have shotguns and ducks in them—not only day-by-day killing of ducks for food, predator-like, but live ducks predominating on the water or in the air, on big marsh or small marsh or slough or open lake.

There was a fair-sized slough that possibly no human being had visited for a week or more. Its surface was covered with ducks of mixed species, divers and dabblers crowded together over acres and acres, right up to the water's edge and on the muddy shore. I made a perfect sneak for nearly a hundred yards, inching up over the ice ridge and down into the bowl of the slough until my face was concealed only by the last fringe of bulrushes. I could not see much of details until I got there, but, once there, I could almost touch ducks. The nearest were sleeping on the mud. Out on the water for a good hundred and fifty yards, ducks sat and fed. Just about every duck species that belonged in South Dakota was in front of me, including—especially—canvasbacks. Canvasbacks were there by the hundreds, from ten yards or less to as far away as I could distinguish them—such special ducks, even then. I was there as a predator as well as a watcher, but I was so engrossed by the sight of the ducks that I botched the hunting. I watched and watched those dark red canvasback heads and necks sticking out among the brownish heads and necks of shovelers and gadwalls and mallards, until finally some duck saw what was upon them, and the whole gathering rose out of there so fast that I had time to line up the gun barrel on only one bird. It turned out to be one of the not-so-delectable shovelers, and I had to undress and wade fifty yards out in the muck after it.

That shoveler was my total bag for that afternoon. I told no one about the fiasco, nor did I do much talking about anything that evening. Over and over, I visualized canvasback heads, their straight lines and curves fitting in with strong necks. The dark, almost blackish, red heads of the drakes had their bright red eyes to focus attention still more. Sometimes, the more I thought of the canvasback heads, the less I could reconstruct the images of other ducks, until, with closed eyes, I could see canvasback heads as if they alone were painted distinctly against an indistinct background.

Some forty years ago, from a duck pass on the old farm, I saw flights of the now-scarce redheads during which I am sure that more redheads passed over or near me in two hours than I have seen all together in the last twenty years. Redhead flocks roaring sixty to eighty yards overhead, a half-dozen flocks abreast at times, and more and more of them coming in, all traveling in the same direction at the same speed and alighting, flock after flock, in the middle of a lake—a spectacle of magnificence that I doubt any man now living will see again on any north-central lake or perhaps anywhere in the world. I do not contend that my memories are without sadness.

The central waters of lakes also had their panoramic views of ducks other than the by-gone wonders of the canvasbacks and redheads. The divers among these other ducks were mostly bluebills and ringnecks, and they gave the appearance of black and white dots on the surface. Flights of bluebills and ringnecks would come in at any hour of day but usually toward evening, sometimes flock after flock dropping out of the sky, gliding and zigzagging, almost tumbling down to splash with outstretched feet. Or they would fly low over the water, bunched up or in spread-out formation. On a rainy or foggy day or evening, a lake might seem to be covered with bluebills and ringnecks. In stormy weather, they might either seek the quieter waters in the shelter of points or islands or hills or wooded stretches of shore or ride the waves of the lake centers. Great rafts of mallards might likewise ride waves or huddle close to shore on stormy days or cover lake centers in calm weather. But these are not sights only of the past. We may see their equivalents involving the still-common species of ducks on lakes and marshes of today. Some of the state and federal wildlife refuges of the Dakotas still offer much the same sights of ringnecks, bluebills, mallards, pintails, ruddies, baldpates, and teals that I saw when I was young.

My choice memories of ducks are not all of panoramas. There were some stand-out sights of just a few ducks or of lone ducks— the first white-winged scoters, the first buffleheads, and the first lone wood duck that I ever saw. (The present has greatly improved

over the past of my early years with respect to wood ducks, for there are undoubtedly far more wood ducks over most of the north-central region today than when I lived on the farm.) There was one oddity: it was the size of a small goose, and had a goose-like bill, green head, white breast, and other markings suggesting hybridization between an American goldeneye and I could not make up my mind what else.

· · · ·

The frosts of the Indian summer nights leave thicker and thicker ice on the ponds in the mornings. In shaded, quiet places, the ice may not melt all day. Where a muskrat swims, there may be a swirl of bubbles and pieces of broken ice film, or the animal travels submerged, breaking the ice film only where it surfaces.

of marshes and fall   41

One evening, needles form a crystalline lacework on the lake-side rocks, the water's edge becomes still and films over, and the lake also, except where the ducks sit. During the night, the new ice film thickens, cracking now and then, with water oozing from the cracks to freeze in turn.

By morning, the coots are gone—all that can fly—and so are the grebes and most of the ducks that do not like ice. There may still be many bluebills and ringnecks out in the remaining open water if the freeze-up is not too hard. Muskrats sit beside open holes. New lodges and feed houses appear over the marshes. Faint, muddy prints of both muskrats and minks mark the new ice. Lake shore ice, in particular, may have a little blood, some bits of vegetation, fish scales or skin about the rocks and openings where minks and muskrats feed. Crows sit out on the ice, pecking and cawing.

With the first freeze-up, mallards typically appear by thousands. They cover the remnants of open water or sit on the ice. If the ice melts again in a day or two, the waterfowl population may not be so much different from before except for the departure of the coots and the mild-weather ducks and for the greater proportions of mallards. More of the ducks have brighter plumage in late fall: the green heads of the mallard drakes are greener, the cinnamon on the heads of the greenwing drakes stands out and so do the white throats and brown necks of the pintail drakes. The drakes of what are locally known as the "northern spoonbills" do not look like the same species as the brownish shovelers of early fall.

Mallards may be in no hurry to leave as long as they have access to cornfields and a safe place to sit between feedings. They may still be on the larger lakes by early winter.

One December, I had a trapping camp on a large island in a lake. Through the Christmas holidays, the weather remained mild, though the lakes and marshes were frozen enough to permit my walking on the ice in the morning, if not during the rest of the day. I have two outstanding memories of that month.

A loon sat in the smaller open spots and fished and called, day and night. In its grayish winter plumage, it blended into its background or flashed its whiter underparts as it stood up beating its wings, or it sank beneath the water and came up again. Sometimes it would swim from one open spot to another beneath the ice.

The other memory is of mallards. An open area of twenty to thirty acres, situated less than a quarter-mile from camp, was packed with the mallards, a danger-tempered group that knew about all that mallards needed to know to live. For weeks, most of them did not leave to feed in the cornfields before dark. At all times of night, their quacking and restless flying could be heard—every few minutes punctuated by a roar as hundreds or thousands got up, to alight again. Minks dragged over the ice the bodies of the lead-poisoned or crippled birds that sat or lay about the outskirts of the flock, but the main group lived with security from predatory enemies, including myself.

•　　•　　•

On a north-central marsh or lake, the final encroachment of ice may leave the remaining water crowded with ailing ducks and coots and with the indubitably functional goldeneyes and mergansers to which hanging about the last open water is a way of their lives. Birds that I enjoy watching are the little hooded mergansers and buffleheads, with their neat bodies and dark and white contrasts. The big, almost mallard-like American and red-breasted mergansers usually do not permit a close approach. They may circle, fly away, then return almost to drop into the water, then fly away again. Sometimes, a long-necked and long-billed western grebe is among the last occupants. Out at the South Dakota farm, we found one floundering on the ice and tried to help it take wing but nearly got speared doing so.

The migratory users of a water hole may come and go before one even sees them there. While out on the central ice of a marsh studying the "sign" about a strip of open water next to a muskrat lodge, I found myself staring at enormous bird droppings and white contour feathers stuck to the ice. Later, I saw the undoubted source of the droppings and feathers, but on another marsh—a flock of six whistling swans, here too staying about as far from shore as they could. They flew low over the central ice and rushes, rising as they approached shore until high over the big cottonwoods, then leveled off in a straight-away cruising flight.

•　　•　　•

If the real, tight freeze-up comes in fair weather, we may have one great phalanx of mallards after another going by, hundreds of yards overhead. This may be the "northern flight" so long anticipated by the hunting public, and hunters in new hunting clothes may line the hilltops and lake shores—and go home without ducks. It has now become an annual cycle, the blown-up daydreams of the northern flight, when the dubbiest dubs expect to bag their legal limits almost without trying, and the disappointing reality of the actual hunting. The ducks do not want to be shot during the northern flight any more than at any other time, and, unless they are innocents making their first acquaintance with modern man and his firearms, they may not get shot, any more than the ducks preceding them.

Mass movements of ducks in late fall need not be a disappointment to people who are not too preoccupied with shooting or bringing home game. Spectacles of clear skies full of ducks can be among the most imposing in Nature, the glinting of light on white wings and breasts far off to the side, the dark strings and bunches of flying birds to be seen in all directions, even those so distant that the position of a flock may be lost before it is much more than discovered. Add frost to the air, and the person with a capacity for enjoying rare sights may watch and watch and be glad that he lives.

Nor need one always wait until the onset of winter to see the big, high flights—they may sometimes be seen on the mildest of sunny fall days, if one looks for them, away up there, where even buckshot cannot reach. Let those who wish to see things try lying on a lake-side hill, scanning the sky for migrating ducks, geese, hawks, and now and then something more unusual, like a flock of sandhill cranes.

The northern flight may conform most closely to popular ideas when freeze-up comes with a storm. Even then, a hunter has to know how to hunt and how to shoot, if he is to bag ducks, and his opportunities may be variable. If visibility is poor for the ducks, it is also poor for the hunters, and, if the weather is bad enough, the ducks may go right on through, high up and out of range or out of sight—unless bewildered or desperate for rest, food, or water. During a blizzard, mallards may continue to pour into a strategic water hole despite gun fire from the edges, but that is not the kind of hunting that I care for. I always had a notion that ducks should be left alone under such circumstances and that human hunters have no business groping around in a snowstorm among patches of open water and thin ice out in the center of a marsh or lake, good hunting or not.

Let autumn be ended appropriately with a snowstorm, with a

vague moving whiteness turning gray as night approaches, with snow settling down or streaking or swirling in aerial eddies, and the water birds—the healthy and the doomed—sitting on or about the open water. Then, a hardening of the slush, and the birds that can fly disappear into the enveloping snow; the other birds sit or walk or freeze into the slush. To the minks belong the surface as well as the edge of marsh and lake now. The night is a good night for them as they drag booty to their retreats ashore, but that is quite natural and proper. Minks have to eat, too.

5. *of marshes and winter*

For marsh animals adapted to live beneath the ice, early winter may bring no great problems. There are usually weeks after freeze-up on a north-central marsh when the water is of almost uniform temperature and without movement except near springs, stream currents, or where fishes or muskrats disturb it. Its gaseous content does not often change with suddenness, and the foods for the animal life that must feed remain about as available one day as the next. The outside temperatures may vary from forty above zero to forty below without making much difference to the life in the water—as long as the essentials for living remain.

Some individuals may be in as bad a way in early winter as in any other season, but it is hard to think of much of the functional marsh life being helpless under the new ice. As a man walks on inch-thick surface over the shallows, and cracks shoot away with each step, bullheads and fathead minnows also shoot away, almost as part of the radiating cracks. Just at the edge of vision they may go, living slivers of black or silver, with now and then a flickering gleam as a fish flips on its side in getting away. There may be painted turtles and snapping turtles—big, green-backed snappers, still being their own private enterprises but at a slow-motion tempo, crawling over the marsh bottom or hiding in the leafy plants or digging down out of sight, with suspended mud rising and spreading in the water like smoke, over a spot where a snapper disappeared.

With the continued sinking of the frost line, the seeming isolation of aquatic animals from winter's problems may be transformed into a series of patent emergencies. Crises may be of gradual onset or abrupt; their sequences are complex or of direct cause-and-effect relationships. The clear water of marshy shallows naturally freezes before the deeper clear water of the centers, but the mud about cattail rootstocks and some other plant growths may long remain unfrozen. Snowdrifts over emergent vegetation not only impede the freezing, but ice that formed before the drifting may also melt away under the protection of the drifts. At the same time, snow over the ice, by cutting off the sunlight required by submerged plants for photosynthesis, introduces its own complications, such as oxygen depletion and the accumulation of toxic gases.

In the course of a killing freeze-out, the last places on a marsh where fishes keep alive include the plunge holes and channels of muskrat burrows and lodges. The water there may be packed with bullheads; almost all other marsh fishes die before this stage. The bullheads gulp air, trying to live, whether the oxygen is all gone from the water or not, whether the water reeks with hydrogen sulfide or not. A few die, or many may, and the living wriggle among masses of floating dead.

Minks respond to the dying and dead fishes in or about the muskrat retreats, as they do to the availability of crayfishes, large insects, and frogs. The muskrats may or may not feed upon fish, depending principally upon whether they have access to an abundance of choice plant foods, to rootstocks or tubers of cattails, bulrushes, reeds, or duck potatoes. When the better plant foods are in short supply, the muskrats may feed upon the fishes almost to the extent that the minks do, either upon the victims they obtain by themselves or upon those dragged out and left by the minks. The stomachs of nearly half of one sizable lot of midwinter muskrats from a northern Iowa marsh contained bullhead flesh.

When substantial flows of water enter a marsh that has been long covered by thick ice and snow, the local massing of the fishes may be conspicuous. These fishes may be minnows or they may be big ones or of all sizes. Their packed bodies may have a volume of less than a cubic foot or up to dozens of cubic yards. They may make the water seethe with bodies or gulping mouths, or an observer may not be able to see much of any life by looking from above into openings in the ice.

Sometimes, for not wholly apparent reasons, a patch of water may not freeze over, or its ice covering opens up, and a person may stand at the edge and watch bullheads come and go. The underwater stems and leaves and filaments remind me of seaside depths in miniature; the swimming bullheads, of small sharks down there among the colors and shadows. The bullheads are but indistinct shapes, they swim boldly into clear spaces, they blend again into underwater patterns. They may lie quietly, a few or many in sight. Here may come a big one, or it gradually takes form as an outline drawing against a gray background of depths. Sometimes, watching, I feel a momentary skin-prickling despite realities.

• • • •

The muskrats, not being as dependent upon the water as the fishes, have more leeway in meeting freeze-out crises, but they can winter-kill. As a rule, those living in food-rich environment having little water get along better than those in food-poor environment having more water. In the shallows that are grown to cattails and bulrushes, the muskrats can still dig out nutritious underparts, even though considerable freezing of the bottom muck occurs.

If the muskrats are forced to come out on the surface to feed in cold weather, some of them may still find something edible in the exposed plant crowns and rootstocks. They gnaw the favored parts right down into the ice and may almost stand on their heads, hindquarters braced above, as they tug and twist. They eat the river bulrush rootstocks sticking here and there from the outside of a lodge. The gnawed pieces of rootstocks show their tooth grooves wherever the feeders reached up from the surface of the ice or climbed up on a lodge. But the muskrats are not the very best of climbers, and a hungry one that overextends itself on a steep surface may slip or tumble down.

When the entire food supply of the muskrats becomes encased in ice—as is often true where nothing but coontail and other submerged water plants occur in a foot or two of water, and all of this freezes to the bottom—their situation becomes one of deadly crisis almost in a matter of hours. They cut out through the sides of lodges to travel over the ice, going from one frozen lodge to another, gnawing at the fish frozen in the plunge holes or upon the vegetation making up the lodges. They fight with and eat upon the bodies of their fellow muskrats or leave the marsh to wander over the countryside—tails, eyes, and feet freezing, always vulnerable to whatever predators prey upon muskrats that are trying to live at a hopeless disadvantage.

Here is a beaten group trying to weather a cold snap. They huddle, a half dozen of them, in the eaten-out and reworked shell of a small lodge. Some openings to the outside are plugged with mud, fragments of waterlily rootstocks, and miscellaneous debris, even with frozen bodies of bullheads. Other openings are partly plugged; others are not plugged at all, and inside the muskrats sit with upper parts frosting and lower parts wet. The inside ice-glaze has bullhead bodies in it but the muskrats are no longer eating bullheads. They are no longer doing anything except sitting or rearranging themselves. A wet tail tip sticks out of an opening and freezes to the ice outside. I have stroked the backs of such animals with a hatchet handle, and they just turned to look at me, without otherwise moving.

Next morning, the whole top of the lodge shell is open, empty of muskrats, and powdered by a trace of snow. A mink-killed muskrat lies smeared with blood on the ice, and a drag trail represents another victim. A third muskrat lies on the ice without a wound on it but with lungs congested from pneumonia. The trail of a live muskrat can barely be distinguished; after tracking around the wreckage of the lodge, the animal headed for shore, where it worked the rushy and weedy fringes before crawling under a boat. The muskrat tail tip is still frozen to the ice beside the lodge, but the rest of the animal is gone. Fox tracks center about this spot, and they lead off in a straight line toward shore. A crow alights by the mink-killed muskrat; after a little pecking, it walks over to feed on a big bullhead that somehow got on the ice away from the lodge. The mink returns to its remaining victim of the night, but the blood-saturated underfur is now frozen too solidly to the ice for the mink to wrench it free. The mink finally drags away the muskrat with the pneumonic lungs, following the same drag trail it had made earlier.

When something is wrong with a wintering muskrat population in the north-central region, the animals tend to be active on the surface of the ice. The better situated a wintering population is, the less day-by-day external evidence it usually leaves, except for new repairs in lodges and burrows. Under normal conditions, minks repeatedly dig into the lodges, and the muskrats, as repeatedly, plug the holes from within after the minks leave. Or, the muskrats abandon the less favored lodges—with mink holes in them or not—or rehabilitate them later, if for any reason they need to do so or feel like doing so.

There are different degrees of security in wintering muskrat populations of glacial marshes, even where practically all individuals are able to survive. Some have to do little except sit, sleep, swim, feed, and show a minimum of wariness toward the more ill-disposed of their fellow muskrats and their racial enemies, the intruding minks. Others have to work hard for their lives, as the ice thickens and the water recedes under the ice. Some live in dry passageways and run along dry trails between nests and feeding sites. Thaws cause the flimsier structures to collapse, or the ice or snow melts about the pushed-up plugs of vegetation, mud, stones, and sticks over the burrows; and then the occupants have more problems of repairs. Plugging of openings may go to extremes, as when a muskrat continues to push wet vegetation through a small hole to the cold outside, and, with each new push, a horn of vegetation protrudes farther on the outside until it topples over from its own weight.

In cutting through ice, the muskrats are adept if they work from below, and they may work well at this in water. They may gnaw upward through the ice in the middle of a marsh, and then heap up the vegetation for a new lodge around the new hole. I happened to be walking across the bare ice of a marsh center when a muskrat cut through ahead of me. It pulled its wet body out, and there it sat amid ice splinters beside a hole leading down through a foot or so of ice. A muskrat may similarly gnaw from below the ice over the plunge hole of a solidly frozen, abandoned lodge and rehabilitate the lodge in a few hours.

Muskrats do have a behavioristic weakness in working with ice in that they seldom display much ability to gnaw *downward* to open up a passageway to the water. During periods of extensive winter-wandering, they cut through the walls of unoccupied lodges or into feed houses, push-ups, or ice-heaves, to take shelter over frozen plunge holes or to gnaw on plant and animal materials lying about, but there they often die of cold without making any progress in reaching the comparative safety of the water beneath. I have found wanderers (perhaps a little thin and bleeding from a few minor strife wounds, yet not in wretched condition) lying dead over plunge holes sealed by no more than a few inches of newly frozen ice—and with indications that the victims knew the locations of the plunge holes without being able to take advantage of them.

Exposure of their bare extremities—including eyes—to freezing temperatures would delimit their above-ice activities, but they do not seem to have noticeably better luck in regaining access to water beneath the ice in mild weather, unless their efforts are facilitated by melting of ice or frozen mud.

A heavy thaw imposes its own problems upon a muskrat population that got along well in the labyrinths of layered ice and subsurface channels left by receding water during cold weather. The pouring of water from above does not necessarily endanger muskrats through drowning, for only under exceptional conditions are north-central muskrats unable to reach air; but they may need to do some quick adjusting when forced out on the surface of land or ice or into the upper parts of previously unmaintained lodges and burrow systems. At such times, many of the animals are briefly vulnerable to minks and other predators or are subject to attacks of other muskrats if the emergency forces more intimacy than muskrats are disposed to tolerate, particularly as the spring breeding season approaches. If a cold snap follows the thaw while the muskrats are still in process of adjusting to the flood waters, their troubles are compounded. The luckier of the unlucky ones get by with only frozen tails.

• • •

The lesser creatures under the marsh ice—the numerous kinds of water bugs and water beetles, the dragonfly and damselfly nymphs, the small crustaceans, the leeches, the mollusks—gradually approach states in which an observer may hardly judge whether they are alive or dead. A motionless specimen from oxygen-deficient water may move when transferred to tap water or it may never move again. Masses of invertebrates may, like fishes, collect at strategic places under the ice. Once, after chopping ice that covered a water hole at a trapping camp, I dipped out several pails of the misnamed water scorpions—harmless but bizarre in appearance and something to see when looked at by the pailful!

At the edge of the marsh, some forms of life are out of reach of a sinking frost line, others are adapted to withstand it, and the others die when conditions become intolerable. Crayfishes die in their burrows, and there may be dying of frogs, toads, mice, and shrews—though it should not be assumed that all of this mortality must be due to frost. A short distance away, in the higher ground, the impersonal frost overtakes some of the wintering garter snakes, some to die and some to lose only their tail tips.

•   •   •

Outside, the snow blows across bare ice. Little drifts collect in the lee of the rough spots, to blow away again and to rebuild. The water welling out of a new ice crack catches blowing snow, and the new little drift spreads and freezes. Elsewhere over the ice, the remaining snow may be in the trails of mink or fox or jackrabbit. Here, the once-soft snow that packed under their feet persists as little raised spots after the loose snow blows clear.

Drifts collect over marshy growths of cattails and bulrushes and reeds and over the weeds and brush of the shore zones. Hard particles hiss over old sun-crusts on the surface of ice and snow. Anvils of snow overhang the steeper banks, up to ten to fifteen feet in height, sometimes so fluffy that a man could drop out of sight in one. Or long, smooth drifts of almost ice-like hardness extend from shore far out on the ice of marsh or lake. Muskrat lodges disappear beneath the snow covering, or tops or sides stick out, dark patches against the whiteness. The snow may play in smoky wisps, or swirl and settle, burying or partly burying, exposing or partly exposing.

Dust may blow with the snow, and depressions left by wild feet drift over flush with the surface again, each one filled with gray rather than white snow. Trails of gray dots lead off out of sight— the two-by-twos or three-by-threes or four-by-fours of mink, the nearly straight line-up of fox tracks, and the forked patterns of rabbit, marking every stop and turn. The mouse and shrew trails or the prints of small birds may take the dust stenciling like the larger trails. When the sun warms, the small dust-marked trails become distorted into bigger ones. The snowdrifts may become mud drifts, and new tracks appear in both mud and wet snow.

The thickening ice turns pale or remains dark; it is clear or full of air or gas bubbles; it is crisscrossed by cracks or blotched by yellowish upwellings or powdered with dust to focus the sun's rays and melt the surface. Evaporation brings up the once-submerged leaves and stems of waterlilies and the coontails and pondweeds and the dead fishes, and these focus the sun's rays for new melting. Melt waters of thaws freeze on the surface, smoothing it over again, or ice masses unattached to the bottom rise above the new water, rougher and crustier on top than before.

When the ice cracks again and again along the same lines, the scars enlarge with each successive freezing until they are an inch or more wide—many inches wide on the larger lakes and marshes. The outward push of the ice may break off the point of a peninsula in late winter, at times moving acres of shallow marsh bottom and rocky shore. Earthen ridges some feet in height may be pushed up around the edges of even the smaller marshes if the ice gets a good hold of movable mud or sand. Fallen trees, docks, boats, or fences that the ice gets hold of at the edge of the water break against the ridges. If the ice is sufficiently well contained in the bowl of a body of water, or if its expansion is sufficiently irregular, it may buckle out away from shore. On northern waters, one may see jumbled ice fields and shoreline heaps of five-foot ice.

The movements of the ice may break the rootstocks of cattail or waterlily. They may crush and mangle and disrupt. Some things adjust to it and some things do not. The ice, as a manifestation of cold, operates impersonally, always. An air-gulping group of bull-heads may survive the winter in the unfrozen water of an abandoned muskrat burrow under a lake bank but stay there to die in the spring or summer if the ice cuts off their passageway back to the lake. Likewise, the same ice may seal up a "hotspot" burrow system having muskrats dead from epidemic disease, in such a way that newcomers are unlikely to enter, to contract the disease in their turn.

· · · ·

Winter cold on the north-central prairies can be anything from benign to unendurable to all forms of life exposed to it. At one extreme are the thaws, with spiders and crayfishes crawling over wet ice; at another, the brittle tightness of cold under which ice splits and booms continuously.

Great cold—by which I mean thirty or forty degrees below zero Fahrenheit, or colder—is generally accompanied by calm air. Frost gathers on beards, eyebrows, fur, outer garments, buildings, trees, or on the ice or snow. Breath comes from a man's mouth or from a horse's nostrils in vapory spumes. The skin on one's face draws tight, and the sides of one's nose and cheeks prickle and harden. The cold may hurt and benumb and bear down like a tangible weight. One may wonder just how much might be endured, just where the danger line lies after feet go dead. But any kind of cold is milder without wind than the same cold with wind. With wind, great cold becomes something that a man cannot face more than momentarily nor can many other vertebrates, including natives of the northern plains and prairies, winter-tested over millions of years.

In northern Minnesota, I walked out of the shelter of a woods-fringed river into the sweep of a strong wind coming off a lake at probably fifty to fifty-five below zero. The sensation that I knew, as the wind hit my face, was like that of a burn. Even the bison cannot endure that sort of weather without shelter, and winter-active wildlife in general holes up or beds down or gets behind something when conditions become overly severe.

There is, however, much variation in the responses of wildlife to great cold. Chickadees continued to be active in some of the coldest daytime weather that I was ever out in, but they just about have to do their usual daily feeding to live. They fluff themselves into the softest of balls and call "dee-dee-dee-dee-ee," whether they squat low on the branches or flit about. Rabbits feed during periods of great cold, but they also spend much time in holes or bedded down in snow and vegetation. Coyotes, foxes, weasels, goshawks and rough-legged hawks, horned and snowy owls take most of what comes in the way of cold weather. Weasels are active in the open air at much colder temperatures than their bigger relatives, the minks. Minks may not emerge from snowdrift or subsurface retreats at all during weeks of unrelieved great cold as long as they can live comfortably where they are. The behavior of striped skunks may show anomalies; the skunks may hibernate for months during mild winters, yet an individual may work the snowdrifts and shore lines and mink-opened muskrat lodges and the bases of fence posts across a field in severe weather, without evidence of detriment from so doing.

In some cases, it is hard to judge why an animal succumbs to cold, whether it is the intensity of the cold, alone, or of cold superimposed upon hunger. Where a bobwhite covey roosting in a snow-filled, marsh-edge plum thicket leaves a starved bird or two dead on the roost, the story may be quite plain, especially if the survivors have feeble powers of flight and stuff themselves on such innutritious fare as rose fruits and buckbrush berries. If a dead screech owl be found during a cold snap, its stomach empty but its body in fair flesh, one may not conclude much more than that it is dead. The northward pioneering of raccoons in recent years— approaching or passing the classic Fifty-third Parallel in Manitoba

—brings up questions as to how much hunger and intense and prolonged cold this southern species can endure. In the case of the opossum, there is less cause to question—many are found dead by spring in central Iowa and southern Wisconsin, and many of the survivors have noticeably emaciated bodies and frost-stubbed tails and ears.

•　•　•

One does not actually see so many forms of life on a north-central marsh in midwinter. By then, all waters except the swiftest streams, the biggest lakes, and the warmest spring holes are sealed over, and the last of the ducks and coots are either gone or dead. Occasionally, some mallards or mergansers are to be seen in flight, or a kingfisher stays all winter if it finds a place where it can always feed, but the common species living above ground or ice or snow are those that belong there.

Short-eared owls fly waveringly over marsh and over land in late afternoon and twilight, and, higher in the air, rough-legged hawks circle or hover, bodies poised and wings beating. In some years, snowy owls come down from the North, to sit on fence posts or muskrat lodges or haystacks or out on the ice. They may be tame or wary, these strangers that still belong. The goshawk is another visitor from the North, as big and powerful as the redtail but adapted for sprint-flying rather than soaring. It hunts in the woods and in the open; it may sit on a killed pheasant at the edge of a plum thicket and allow a man to walk almost up to it, or it may fly straight away with a speed suggested only by the rapidity with which its body grows smaller to view. In its compact power, it is a bird wonderfully adapted to its way of life.

In a willow thicket, a tiny saw-whet owl may sit with such unsophistication that one person may distract it while another sneaks behind to capture it by hand. Willow thickets may also have their short-eared owls, and, sometimes, their long-eared owls, as well. On occasion, thickets are full of the owls of one or the other of the latter two species. Owls may sit on their roosts or fly off in all directions. The ground or snow beneath the roost trees may be littered with owl castings, with here and there bunches of small feathers and tufts of mouse fur. I never have been able to make out any constant rules as to which of these owls will occupy the thickets, but it usually is one species and not the other, with

the shortears being birds more of marshy and open land than are the longears.

As a marshland owl, the great horned owl dominates in winter as much as it does at any other time. If it wants to stay in the woods, it does so. If it wants to hunt over marsh or field, it does so. It leaves prey remains or castings under vine tangles or leafy oak trees or fence posts or on muskrat lodges or wherever it can sit down. It preys upon what is most conveniently caught and handled, which usually means rabbits, sometimes mice. Now and then, it preys upon almost any animal life coming outside in winter, up to skunks and foxes, and including minks and weasels, pheasants and quail, woodpeckers, and any smaller owls. Within the limitations imposed by pestiferous crows, by the territorial intolerances of other horned owls, by man, and by availability of food, this formidable though unimaginative predator does much as it pleases.

of marshes and winter   57

In the old days, prairie chickens roosted in the sedges and thick grasses around the marshes of eastern South Dakota and fed in the surrounding cultivated fields. I remember their bursting out of unbroken snow at my feet and their feeding on cold mornings on the buds of lakeshore cottonwoods. There might be evening flights of these birds strung out in mile-wide flocks, flying at the height of country-line telephone wires and sometimes leaving some dead beneath the wires. During blizzards, I would also encounter prairie chicken flocks in the lee of strawstacks, and they would even come into our farmyard.

The late afternoon flights of crows in the direction of evening roosts may be seen against settings of coloring sky and snow marked with shadows and red and gold. There is an easy purposefulness in these movements. The crows fly leisurely enough and sometimes they stop enroute in a field to feed, and long lines of crows in the air and on the ground have their stragglers. Their performance is one of adequacy. The crows know what they are doing and get it done with what they have to do it with—adequately. Theirs are not the screaming wings of the peregrine falcon, nor can they dart through brush like a goshawk or one of the lesser bird-hawks, nor do they have a repertoire of fancy tricks in flight. Their wings serve to transport them from place to place, and they flap along, being birds in their own right.

The behavior of crows differs much under differing circumstances, from the quiet strict-attention-to-business of a lone crow working hungrily on a carcass to the sentinel-like activities of certain individuals of a big flock. They may mob a great horned owl with practically human animosity, giving their fullest measure to the job, following the owl from tree to tree as it flies, circling and diving and sitting around in an uproar of cawing, buffeting it on head or back until it snaps beak and hoots or launches forth in pursuit of one of its pesterers. A smaller owl or a hawk also draws crows, but the excitement of the crows is less likely to be intense, and their mobbing of the lesser birds of prey may be perfunctory. As thousands of farmers and hunters have observed, the tameness of crows toward unarmed persons and their exaggerated respect for anyone having a gun in sight should be evidence enough of the powers of discrimination of a bird that has learned to live with man and has intentions of continuing to do so.

Crows see a great deal of the organic matter that appears on the surface of ground, snow, or ice. They dig at grasshopper egg-cases on a hillside, or peck at a hunter-killed duck or coot or at a dead chicken or pig thrown out by a farmer, or feed on ear corn, or pick grain out of cattle dung. Their pecking on the ice may be at the sites of frozen-over springs, where entrapped bodies of fishes are becoming exposed at the surface, or at remains of almost anything unlucky—skunk, mole, muskrat, crayfish—that could wander around out there to die.

•   •   •

The winter-active mammals that one sees most in daylight about the marshes are jackrabbits and cottontails. The jacks sit in cattail clumps or in dug-out snowdrifts and bound away when alarmed. They stop and stand upright on hind legs to look back, then bound onward again. The cottontails like to sun themselves in protected places, and, when abundant, their darker bodies are to be seen against the snow all around the shore zone and sometimes out in the marsh. In the old days in South Dakota, they sat next to thickets, and, when I needed meat, I had no trouble approaching within thirty yards of them, to shoot as many as wanted, one after another. Now, in Iowa, they are so hunter-wise that they usually sit beside holes in the ground or in deep drifts, and a hunter may hardly approach one openly without seeing it go into a hole—sometimes with insulting leisureliness at distances of a hundred and fifty yards or more! Or, far ahead, they may run over a hill or circle widely about the hunter, and, if followed with any persistence, they, too, go into holes.

When the marsh and the surrounding lands are full of meadow mice, their forms dart among the ground litter and plant growths, and the flesh-eaters respond to them in their own ways. The quartering, circling, hovering, and dropping of the short-eared owls and the mouse-hunting types of hawks are common sights. A red fox smells, listens, waits, pounces, and scratches at the ground or snow. One may see a weasel bounding back and forth, or, in mild weather, a hunting raccoon.

I like to watch minks as much as any of the marsh dwellers, although opportunities for direct observations of minks are variable. One may spend day after day for months on a marsh without seeing a mink, then see minks every day for several days. Sights of minks may be only of an animal running along the shore or sticking its head out of a hole in a muskrat lodge. It is more of an event when a mink stands erect on hind feet to look, or maybe to approach out of curiosity, alternately running back and returning. To that extent, it shows its kinship with the weasels, but I never have known any mink to be quite as curious and bold as the weasels. I had a short-tailed weasel come up to me while I sat on a log beside a marsh writing field notes, to run up my leg and up my arm to my shoulder while exploring my person. The most boldness a free wild mink ever showed me was to snatch from my hands some of its food that I was examining at the entrance of its den. In another instance, a screaming mink jumped toward my face as I looked into a hole in the top of a muskrat lodge.

●   ●   ●

It is by "reading sign," rather than by direct observation, that the wintering fortunes of marsh creatures are best followed under ordinary conditions. The "sign" may be faint—covered by blown snow or distorted by the sun or it may be just a little blood or fur or some tracks on smooth ice that one has to squint along the surface to see—or it may be tracks fresh-frozen in slushy snow and datable to the hour. It may be the accumulated frost at the entrance of a skunk den. It may be the battle ground of a couple of big minks messing up hundreds of square yards of surface. It may be a place where foxes pawed around an object having human scent on it—on one occasion, they dug up a lost hatchet for me.

Tragedies furnish some of the more notable "sign." A mole, becoming lost after leaving the unfrozen ground under a drift, is unable to dig back into the ground elsewhere; it walks on top and it burrows through the snow, around and around, finally to lie dead. Another insectivore, a shrew, may be the lost creature, far out on what is for it a tract of foodless ice, to die, like the mole, because it can do nothing else. Through combined hunger, cold, and smothering snow, a blizzard may kill pheasants, quail, wintering meadowlarks, mourning doves, flickers, and many kinds of smaller birds.

The minks are the specialists in seeking and exploiting dead creatures. They are adept at detecting the scent of the dead as it penetrates to the outside from snowdrift or muskrat lodge or burrow. They are also sufficiently good diggers to break through many frozen surfaces and they can eat away the accessible flesh of coots, ducks, and muskrats partly imbedded in ice.

At times of muskrat die-offs, many nose-hunting predators and scavengers besides minks seek out the dead in lodges, under snow, and even under ice, but they may not have the mink's ability to dig through much frozen material. I have marked the frozen marsh edge where foxes repeatedly tracked and scratched during the winter, and, when the ice melted, there beside the marker was a dead muskrat. The larger and stronger coyotes do better than foxes at opening frozen lodges, and so may the wolves on northern wilderness marshes. Badgers, bears, raccoons, dogs, and even pigs may work over the lodges they can break into if they learn that good scavenging is thus to be had. These others, nevertheless, are usually small-time operators compared with the minks.

That the north-central marshes really belong to the minks during the winter months is manifested in many ways. Minks may prey upon parts of muskrat populations that become vulnerable with the descent of the frost line. The "sign" shows where a muskrat ventured from an opening in the side of a frozen lodge, to make futile explorations about other frozen lodges. After tracking up new snow with its walking, digging, and gnawing, it began its return trip. Then the walking trail changed to a bounding trail that was joined by the trail of a big mink. The two animals rolled as the mink seized the muskrat by neck or shoulder, grappled with forelegs, and kicked and clawed with hind feet. On the snow is blood and a little fur. A dragging trail leads away across the open spaces, through the cattails and bulrushes and reeds, through marginal weed patches, between and over snowdrifts. Partly blown away in the wind, partly drifted over, the trail leads past one open lodge after another, then into a hole, several hundred yards from the site of the killing. A slightly older drag trail, likewise ending at the hole, back-tracks to a place where mink and muskrat wrestled over the snow outside of another lodge. A couple of still older drag trails (but still datable to the same day or to the night before) lead to the same mink's cache of muskrat victims.

Within a week or so after the onset of a deadly freeze-out, the muskrat population of a marsh may be classed as either the dead or the safe—safe, that is, until the descent of the frost line reaches another stage or something else goes wrong. The activities of the minks soon switch from those of predators to those of scavengers. The minks may visit their caches for weeks or they may never return to them. The usual picture on Iowa marshes, however, is one of close utilization of the mink caches by spring.

One type of mink predation that can be conspicuous even at

times of favorable wintering conditions for the muskrats is centered upon certain individual muskrats that show restlessness with the approach of the spring breeding season. The relatively few individuals of the well-situated population that start coming out on the surface of the ice during early-or midwinter thaws, and persist in doing so for any reason, have limited life expectancies, whether their predatory enemies be minks, foxes, dogs, coyotes, or birds of prey. These unhappy or restless individuals vary from full-fleshed animals of either sex at their peak of physical prowess to the thin and chewed-up social misfits of either sex that almost every muskrat population has. They include the senile or the mere "kits"— the last-born young of the last breeding season. They include trap cripples, the sick, or members of the usual surplus of males. They may not fall in any handy classification except that they are muskrats living dangerously while most of the local muskrats are living securely. When these individuals are sooner or later killed off by the opportunistic predators that can do it, or die from fight wounds inflicted by other muskrats, or are otherwise eliminated, the musk- rats of a marsh may again be classed as the dead and the safe— and the period of safety for the safe part of a muskrat population may extend far past the spring break-up and the dispersal from wintering to breeding quarters, the presence of muskrat-hungry and enterprising minks notwithstanding.

For, although it can rightfully be said that a marsh in winter belongs to the minks as much as this can be said of any nonhuman marsh dweller, such does not mean that the minks exert a complete and successful despotism over the other life of the marsh. It may be emphasized that even the much-relished muskrats do not by any means need to allow minks to prey upon them whenever and wherever the minks please. Whole muskrat populations again and again demonstrate their security from minks when living in good environments at comfortable population levels, even with large numbers of minks constantly seeking opportunities to eat muskrats. With advantages in their own favor, the muskrats may even attack and drive off minks, not only when attacking in groups but also singly. Indeed, the course of events in an encounter between a mink and a muskrat away from water depends in part upon whether the muskrat runs or tries to run from the mink or whether it faces the mink, especially when backed into a narrow passageway or into a protecting hole. A mink's eye-view or a mink's mind-image of an unsubmissive large muskrat consisting prominently of incisor teeth is understandably conducive to a substitute diet of frogs or fishes or frozen coots.

The minks usually do have the frogs, the fishes, or the frozen coots, or something else to eat, such as the meadow mice that live in muskrat lodges or run back and forth over snow trails. There are the cottontails and pheasants and smaller creatures of the marsh edge, something dead, something handicapped, something unlucky somewhere, and the minks have the stamina to range over much of the countryside when hungry.

The minks are quite unable to do anything about some wild animals of marshes in winter. If foxes and minks show antagonisms to be read from "sign," the minks are the ones that clearly do the withdrawing to the more foxless parts when withdrawing is done, and the minks may still more clearly avoid the parts regularly frequented by larger members of the dog family.

And, to a very large extent, what individual minks do may depend upon what other individual minks do. The social intolerances of the species become accentuated as mink populations reach the levels at which too many mink-to-mink encounters occur to permit further increases of minks in a given marsh or lake chain. Whether these encounters culminate in bloodless withdrawals or in savage —even deadly—fighting, the freedom of free-living minks is always in relation to what minks have to live with, in winter as at any other season. Living with what they have is what they do, on top of or inside the snowdrifts, while bounding along shore or following a trail in the rushes or fishing from a muskrat plunge hole.

6. *of marshes and marshes*

Although the northern prairie marshes are mainly of glacial origin, they are not exclusively so. There are also the river oxbows. Much of my own experience with oxbows has been along the upper stretches of the Missouri and Mississippi Rivers and their tributaries in Wisconsin, Iowa, and South Dakota—where ducks are still ducks and muskrats still muskrats despite the differences between glacial and oxbow marshes.

At least during the summer months, the ducks of these oxbows run more to the wood ducks that favor such places. The woods bordering the oxbows have the horned and barred owls hooting in the dusk, as do the woods about the glacial marshes of the prairies, but there are usually more of the barred owls about the oxbows. Even in oxbows having the familiar bulrushes, cattails, waterlilies, arrowheads, muskrat lodges, and mink-tracked borders, the plant and animal life of Iowa's big-river oxbows looks a bit more southern—with sycamores and buttonbushes and egrets and turkey vultures and red-shouldered hawks—more like Missouri or Maryland and southward.

•   •   •

The real South has its real marshlands, however much they may differ from the marshes of the North. Once, at New Year's, I walked the edge of a great Louisiana marsh. It certainly had ducks and muskrats, hunters and trappers, and the unmistakable features of a marsh. But, to me, it had its unfamiliar or not-quite-familiar vegetation, the strangeness of smoke of many marsh fires, nearness of the sea, and talk of alligators, red wolves, and enormous turtles and garfishes.

In the late twenties, I spent part of April in southern Georgia and northern Florida with H. L. Stoddard, the ornithologist. I was content to tag along behind him, with confidence that he knew where we were, where we were going, and when and how we would get there. We waded in walking clothes through marshes and swamps, avoiding the cottonmouths and poison ivy on the cypress knees. We lay on the bank where the Wakulla River welled out of the ground, watching the stratification of schools of fishes far, far down in the water of the great spring pool. An everglade kite with its specialized hooked beak fed upon the big snails that are its total diet. There were those large rail-like birds, the limpkins, in the shore vegetation of the flowing river. There were the an-hingas, or snake birds, well enough named when they swam with heads out of the water, but, in the air, resembling flying sticks still more. Out on the Gulf sat the same bluebills and ringnecks and red-heads and pintails and miscellaneous ducks that would soon be heading northward; but there were also the egrets and ibises and brown pelicans and, at night, the calls of chuck-wills-widows.

No muskrats lived for hundreds of miles in what looked like fairly suitable environment—no muskrats much nearer than the coastal marshes of Mississippi or North Carolina or the foot-hills of the Smokies. There were the so-called round-tailed musk-rats—not really muskrats to anyone who knows muskrats. The roundtails were animals with the same fundamental rights of life of other animals. They belonged where they lived—they had what adaptations they needed to maintain themselves, and I was glad that they were there—but they were southerners in a South that I admittedly did not know. The South was genuine, beautiful, and fascinating, but it was not home to one born and apprenticed in a country molded by ice sheets.

●　　●　　●

Desert marshes afford great contrasts in life and lifelessness and, sometimes, in life and death.

In Utah, the Bear River marshes and other marshy areas are formed as fresh stream waters spread out over the flats along the east side of Great Salt Lake, and these have concentrations of water birds. For square mile after square mile, the mid- and late summer scenes are those of wading, swimming, or loafing water birds.

On Iowa marshes and sloughs, one may see, on rare occasions, big shore birds like avocets. In the Dakotas and the Nebraska sandhills, these birds may be abundant enough to be of the species characteristic of most places suitable for shore birds. On the Bear River flats and the flats extending southward, they occur in such abundance that thousands are frequently in sight from one spot. Before visiting Utah, I doubt that I had seen more than a dozen of those preposterously long-legged black and white shore birds, the stilts. South of Bear River, at Ogden Bay, I saw a tract of perhaps ten acres covered with stilts. On the little islands of slightly higher ground away from the channel of Bear River sat family groups of Canada geese, sometimes massed together, sometimes well apart, sitting like large dark lumps or with heads and necks up. Cinnamon and blue-winged teal—indistinguishable to me in their summer plumages—swam and fed and sat almost everywhere, and with them were the mallards, pintails, baldpates, and gadwalls that one expects to find in shallow waters. Diving ducks were there in the proper places—including the waning redheads and canvasbacks. The hundreds of large dark bodies of wading and flying ibises gave a southern aspect to the marshes and flats, but the presence of ravens gave balance in the other direction, and the magpies made it western.

White pelicans came in heavy-beating flocks from their nesting islands in Great Salt Lake, to rest and feed in the waters from Bear River. They launched themselves in flight with a few kicks of their legs, then ascended in slow spirals and leveled off, heading back toward their islands. Here is an ancient stronghold of the species, and their big bones may be seen in the stratified deposits exposed by the flow of Bear River into the salt flats.

There were thousands and thousands of those predatory scavengers, the California gulls—and the terns and grebes and blackbirds and small shore birds. There were muskrats living as muskrats live, in the low river and dike banks and out in the bulrush patches. In response to population pressures, the muskrats were known to disperse away from the choicer or even the livable environments, trying to do something with themselves. Most exceptionally, a muskrat might find a fresh-water spring in which it could stay alive in such an unpromising place as an island in Great Salt Lake, surrounded by miles of brine and desert.

For a field naturalist, one of the delights of the Bear River and associated flats and marshes is the firmness of the bottom. The alternate layers of mud and salt make walking easy except for the slipperiness of the surface mud. I walked in and about bulrush islands a mile or more from shore, to find muskrat lodges built on top of the mud but having entrances dug into the hard substrata.

I do not believe that I ever was actually surfeited by the abundance of living things at Bear River or Ogden Bay, but I came to be no longer impressed by anything less than rarities or multitudes. With clouds of birds getting up ahead of me out on a wet flat and alighting farther ahead or to the rear—the clouds of birds so dense that not much sky could be seen through them in places—lesser abundances seemed like dilutions.

The superlatives of the living extend to death, also. I came to think little of seeing a dead duck or a dead shore bird about wherever I looked—although a dead pelican or three-foot carp was still something to draw attention. Where abundances of animals live, so must abundances die. After about the first week of a visit to the flats, I hardly noticed the dead until dying from botulism became conspicuous.

When possibly fifty dead ducks per acre lie around in a small botulism "hotspot," a person unfamiliar with botulism may think that he is seeing something unusual. The splendid mallards and the priceless redheads lying helpless or dead on mud or water can leave one with a real personal sorrow, but biologists working with botulism at Bear River told me that they would be thankful if the late-summer mortality did not become greatly worse. When hundreds of thousands of ducks die in one season on one area, the dead may line the shores and cover the waters and banks, and they rot, or the gulls leave the carcasses feather-strewn and with the meat eaten away from the breast-bones. And scavengers, the gulls among them, may sicken and die along with the ducks and the shore birds.

These outbreaks of botulism in populations of water birds require special circumstances to become sweepingly deadly: shallow, stagnant, oxygen-poor waters with much decaying plant and animal matter and thriving growths of a particular bacterium. This bacterium produces a toxin that is one of the deadliest of substances for a great variety of living creatures. The ducks that die over botulism waters are not extraordinarily susceptible to the toxin, and many of the sick recover when rescued and transferred to fresh water. For these forms, adapted to live in lowlands though they are, it is a case of "too much is too much." The "too much" can make certain otherwise life-giving marshes outright death traps.

The places that I know to be notorious for their botulism die-offs are in our arid or semi-arid western regions, though botulism *can* kill many ducks elsewhere on the continent. It is in the West that one may count on such mortality occurring in certain areas when occurring at all on any serious scale, but even there it varies with the season and the year. When conditions are right for dying from botulism, there is dying; otherwise, there is not.

•   •   •

My memories of truly desert marshes relate to life and death in two places: Locomotive Springs, north of Great Salt Lake, and the Harney Lake and Malheur Lake area in southeastern Oregon.

At Locomotive Springs, a flow of water appears at the surface of the desert, and down grade from this is a sizable marsh in an area far isolated from other marshes. The marsh has the muskrats and the water birds that belong in marshlands, and, as well as I could judge on the midsummer day of my one visit, they were getting along not much differently from those on other Utah marshes. But the land surrounding the spring and marsh was strewn with dead black-tailed jackrabbits, and deer flies (tabanids) known to be carrying the bacteria of tularemia came forth in a mass attack of such ferocity and persistence that I lost all appreciation for out-door values until I got out of there!

Malheur Lake is a large marsh in the midst of expanses of volcanic dust. It is a breeding ground for common types of water-fowl and a retreat for sandhill cranes. Situated as it is, with its combined vastnesses of wetlands in vastnesses of desert, its attractions for wildlife are understandable. Still working out of the dust of an old Indian camp ground are pieces of native tools and house-hold articles and obsidian arrow heads—sized from big game and war arrows down to the dainty bird arrows—and the bones of practically every species of vertebrate that has lived in the region for centuries. The bone deposits contain remains of thousands of muskrats alone, for the Malheur marshes are muskrat marshes as well as waterfowl marshes.

These marshes, too, can be marshes of death when the botulism bacteria thrive in the decomposing organic debris of the shallows. There are historical accounts of wintering Indians having starved. With countless small black-tailed jackrabbits living about the edge of the wetlands, one may see enough of death even when nothing unusual is happening. Here and there are the leavings of some predator or scavenger. The minks, skunks, and coyotes, the flesh-eating birds, the rattlesnakes, and the occasional bobcat are among the opportunists exploiting the resources of very wet or very dry environments and the life-rich margins that lie between.

The desert closes in on the marsh during years of low water and withdraws again as physical and biological laws require. It remains as impersonal as any other natural phenomenon, habitable to the creatures that are adapted to live in deserts of its kind, uninhabitable to those that are not so adapted.

In years of acute population tensions or crises, the muskrats may move out of the marshes by the hundreds, pouring through dry gullies or across the sagebrush. Their perishing in the desert as a result has its resemblances to the famous movements of lemmings to drown in the Scandinavian seas. Nothing in the way of mysterious impulses or of hereditary betrayals need be postulated to explain muskrat movements into the lethal desert. So far as I can see, these muskrats behave like ordinary muskrats and overflow their home ranges whenever conditions become sufficiently extreme to induce them to do so. Some stay and some leave, and the fact that the ones that leave may end up on a desert should not be unexpected whenever the desert happens to be the place into which movements get started.

Wherever they were, the land routes of mass-moving muskrats that I have examined closely at times of movements were marked by excreta and scent of animals that did not act happy about traveling over unfamiliar and dangerous ground. It is fairly evident how, if the first trails of excited muskrats happen to head off in some direction away from a marsh, the equivalents of main highways become established. About a place like Malheur Lake, more and more muskrats may follow outbound trails until, miles out, fewer and fewer are left alive, to continue wandering while they can.

Sometimes a desert-wandering muskrat does reach safety, but the proportions of muskrats that survive after getting far out on the desert surrounding Malheur Lake must be extremely small. I looked over a spring-watered tract of about four acres of bulrushes on the dry bed of Harney Lake, west of Malheur Lake. There was the mummified carcass of a big muskrat, the "sign" of which could be dated to the previous fall, winter, and spring. It had crossed ten miles or more of desert, to live out its life by itself in about the only place in sight where a muskrat could live. There it lived with everything it needed for its own survival, in a marsh having its own gulls and shore birds and blackbirds, its coyotes and hawks, and some short-eared owls, together with jackrabbits from the rabbit-filled desert.

•   •   •

The plants and animals of desert springs vary with the mineral contents and temperatures of their waters and with the other factors governing amount and distribution of life. Desert springs are occupied, in short, by whatever can reach them and live in or about them, as are environmental niches anywhere. Many of the local populations of marsh-dwelling animals must have only the most tenuous hold on life, and something going very wrong may wipe them out completely. But the persistence in some desert springs of those animals that are unadapted to withstand drought exposure or great concentrations of salts or excessive muddying of the water may be notable. Some of the now-isolated springs about our western deserts have their own distinctive fishes, the remnants of populations that were widely distributed back in Pleistocene time. The modifications that the fishes of these springs have undergone after isolation from their parent stock, during the best-known of our geological epochs, afford a means of measuring rates of evolution in Nature.

I have seen in my lifetime some of the emergencies that droughts bring to wetland wildlife in the course of the more ordinary short-term climatic fluctuations—including emergencies that are not necessarily confined to real desert regions.

In the late thirties, my wife and I made a summer camp in western South Dakota. We were traveling through and picked a place away from the highway where quiet pools were fringed with sedges and bulrushes, and "sign" of green-winged teal and coyote was to be seen in the mud around the pools. It was genuinely "West River" and had its own wilderness beauty, but there was something very literally in the air that was not right—dust, dust-bowl dust, and we did not know what to expect of it. In the afternoon, we had driven off to the side of the road to let a rolling front of dust clouds pass. Then, the air cleared somewhat. By evening, the weather was looking noncommittal, as if the dust storm might be over or might not be.

The dust storm started up again in the night, worse than ever, and we knew that we had better be getting out of there if we could. As I heaved equipment into the car, I felt as if someone were shoveling dirt on my head and neck, and, in the car, we had to await lulls in the wind in order to drive. While the dust poured past, we could barely see that the headlights were on. We reached an inland town, took a room in a small hotel, washed up by lamp light and water pitcher, and looked at each other across the dust-haze, feeling lucky. As we drove on the next day, and looked at the new dust-drifts beside the road, we thought of the quiet rushy and sedgy pools of our abandoned camp ground of the night and wondered if they were still pools.

A mere stage in a drought cycle menaces a wetland area much less than one of the more permanent changes. I remember a camp on the cracked bottom of a once-vast marsh in northwestern Minnesota during the droughts of the thirties. It was enjoyable in its way, for we knew that the marsh would recover in time. We fried steak over a camp fire no more than six inches across, kept continually replenished with short pieces of dry weed stalks while the steak was cooking, and finally extinguished with the greatest thoroughness. The dry marsh might be called a desolation, and perhaps it was, but still a pleasant desolation. The cool air of evening brought a smell of smoke from deep-burning peat into our cruiser tent. We heard night sounds of livings things, of cattle and dogs far off and of rustlings close by, and, at dawn, the hoarse cry of a short-eared owl.

I think also of a lonely Saskatchewan slough, mud-margins encrusted with white salts and the last of the surface water about to disappear, of the howl of a coyote and the unhurried tinkle of a cowbell from a brushy homestead across from our camp. Miles of prairie and plain had no surface waters—ponds and marshes and lakes and streams dry so long that hardly a muskrat burrow remained showing use of recent years. I think of open-mouthed, spread-winged meadowlarks sitting in the shade of fence posts or brush, of tracks of domestic stock, jackrabbits, coyotes, ground-squirrels, mice, snakes, insects, and spiders. I think of clumsy Swainson's hawks eating grasshoppers, of crows, skunks, ground-squirrels, meadowlarks, bullsnakes eating grasshoppers, of dogs and cats from farmyards eating grasshoppers and maybe getting sick from them. And, then, the Qu'Appelle River Marshes, which did not go dry or have their levels seriously lowered in the midst of dried-up southern Saskatchewan. Here were redhead and ruddy and puddle ducks, big Holboell's grebes and muskrats. There was marsh life as well as desert life left in the world, not just one or the other but both. We felt much the same many years later, as—discreetly watching out for rattlesnakes—we sat on high rimrock and looked down upon the wet greenness of an isolated marsh in the volcanic dust country of southeastern Oregon.

On the morning after an Idaho desert camp, we walked a clinkery lava flow that had dammed a valley to form another marsh in an arid region where marshes were not to be seen just anywhere. We had a meal beside that lava-dammed marsh. The lava glistened as if it had only recently spread out to cool, instead of long before any white men ever saw it. The water was fringed with bulrushes and willows. Muskrat cuttings—even out there—lay about feeding places. Broods of ducklings swam in the open. This marsh was more than water and water wildlife in a desert and more than a pleasing combination of colors. It was special, as I saw it, in its manlessness. Nevertheless, one thing in my memory of that marsh does not seem right. When we camped the night before, I kept thinking of what perfect coyote country we were in, but no coyote tracks were to be seen anywhere nor was any coyote singing to be heard.

• • •

In a sense, the sandhill marshes of Nebraska are desert marshes but they are also north-central marshes with typical marsh plants in a setting of sand hills. The sand is bare and drifting in spots, or held by grass, or it is covered by shrubs such as buckbrush and poison ivy, or it has its boxelders and plums growing along creeks and ravines and wherever else they can grow. The low spots have recognizable dirt—muddy when wet—and layers of partly decayed vegetation cover the marsh bottoms, as at other marshes. Away from the water or about the water's edge are the coyotes, skunks, minks, badgers, and bullsnakes, the small sparrow hawks, the western types of soaring hawks, and golden eagles. There are prairie grouse and shore birds where they belong. The ducks are there, and the muskrats.

One does not see the mass spectacles of water birds in the sandhills that one does at Bear River, but the sandhill marshes and their wildlife always leave me with a pleasant feeling. I do not think that they are drainable as long as the water table holds up; the surrounding sand does not invite cultivation; and about the worst abuse that man inflicts upon the country is overgrazing—and at least some of the ranchers are careful to avoid that.

The sandhill muskrats burrow in the sandy soil of the marsh edges, but these burrows, even in places where the sand is fairly well held by plant roots, may be of limited real use. Minks, badgers, raccoons, and coyotes can readily dig down to a nest having young muskrats if they scent its location under the sod. After repeated disturbances, the muskrats of the better marshes have the one workable alternative of keeping their young in lodges out in the wetter parts.

As on the Iowa and Dakota marshes, the predators of the sandhills respond as scavengers when sandhill muskrats suffer heavy losses from disease. Mink droppings passed in the disease "hotspots" contain their high proportions of muskrat remains, and, in winter, coyotes dig into lodges after dead muskrats. And, of course, the muskrats of inferior environments, or those wandering about on dry land far from any secure refuge, are vulnerable to whatever can find and handle them; and the animals dying of hunger, thirst, freezing, or old age become as helpless and as dead in the sandhills as they do anywhere else.

• • •

High mountain marshes may also be desert marshes, though not necessarily because of limited precipitation.

The lower of the mountain marshes—as of Montana, Idaho, or Wyoming—are really on the high plains or in the foothills. They may look, except for surroundings and some details, as if they had been transferred from the eastern Dakotas—or from Utah or Oregon. Some of these marshes about six thousand feet in altitude can be extensive and they may have some special elements in their wildlife. Gray's Lake in southeastern Idaho has its ducks and its muskrats, but it is also a place for sandhill cranes. A hundred miles or so northward of Gray's Lake, at the southern edge of Montana and west of Yellowstone National Park, lie the Red Rock Lakes, a sanctuary of the once-vanishing trumpeter swans. In late summer, swans with cygnets may be seen along the shore zones, while groups of nonbreeders sit out in the open water lake centers, all behaving much as they presumably did centuries ago.

I also thought of the long-ago while watching the ducks in and out from the sedge growths of the shallows about Lower Red Rock Lake. I do not recall ever before having seen quite such concentrations of ducklings in given areas as during a visit in the late forties, not even during my South Dakota youth. It was something to block off in one's mind an acre of open water next to the sedges and to count upwards of twenty-five broods of small ducklings and their mothers swimming and feeding there. For the rearing season, this represented a marsh edge full of ducklings—although, later on in summer or fall, local concentrations of birds capable of flight may greatly exceed such numbers on favored resting or feeding areas almost anywhere along the main flyways.

The old laws of life were still operative in the bird-crowded shallows of the Red Rock Lakes: where there was so much alive, there was death, too. The mink trails on shore were littered with bird remains, and the hundreds of mink droppings in sight consisted mostly of feathers. Also in keeping with the laws of life, the muskrats, which were present in moderate numbers in the shallows, were living without evident losses from the minks. Two family groups of muskrats were found in the vicinity of a den having four or five active young minks. One litter of weaning-age musk-rats was kept only about ten feet away from the mink den. There is no reason to think that minks enjoyed muskrat flesh at Red Rock Lakes less than minks did elsewhere: the muskrats simply appeared to be too well accommodated to be very vulnerable to the minks. Lower Red Rock Lake was, in fact, the highest (almost seven thousand feet) good large muskrat marsh that I ever saw.

At altitudes exceeding eight thousand feet in the northwestern United States, the wetlands reflect increasingly the effects both of terrain and of climate. Marshes tend to lose their bulrushes and cattails, to grade off into willow swamps, bogs, or sedge meadows, and to become more and more dependent for existence upon beaver dams At about nine to ten thousand feet, our northwestern muskrats may find livable environment only in the bigger and deeper and more food-rich of the beaver impoundments. The muskrats are not bashful about eating anything edible that the beavers drag in from surrounding land, and the food habits of muskrats and beavers overlap sufficiently so that the muskrats as a species maintain themselves about as high as the beavers live, though usually in smaller numbers than the beavers in the higher beaver pools.

When disaster in the form of tularemia sweeps the beaver colonies of a mountain stream, it may not only kill the susceptible muskrats at the same time, but the beaver pools may also be lost to the muskrats as the dams wash out or deteriorate through lack of repairs. The beaver pools and associated marshy growths may be short-lived for another reason. With depletion of the surrounding aspens and other staple cold-weather foods of the beavers, the beavers abandon the pools, and the dams come to show the same aspects of disrepair as they would if the beavers had died. If new dams, new pools, and new marshy growths appear elsewhere along the stream to compensate for the loss of the old, then the changes may not make much real difference to the muskrats. But, if beavers become overabundant to the point of wrecking their own food resources all up and down a stream, the muskrats associated with them may find it hard to make adjustments. Hungry beavers make conspicuous inroads into many foods that muskrats eat, including succulent plant roots and almost everything half-way green and tender within reach.

The engineering proclivities of beavers have always been a source of amazement to human observers. An elaborate and functional system of dams, dikes, canals, burrows, lodges, and underwater stores is a remarkable exhibition of a specialized way of life. When something is not right, when the water is too low or the food supply too limited, and the beavers come out to forage in the winter time, there may not be much specialized behavior to see. They leave their trails in the snow, their feeding debris on top of the ice, and their conspicuous water- and mud-splashings (with possibly blood in them) frozen about their passage holes leading under the ice. All of this "sign" may spell out quite elementary responses, like the last living fishes in oxygen-depleted waters gulping air under the ice-heaves.

With beavers in them or not, the beaver impoundments may *make* some of the mountain trout streams. One may look down into a pool and see the trout, big or little, scattered or schooled. They may blend into a background of waterlogged sticks, of disintegrating woody beaver droppings, of plants, and of ripple shadows. The trout may be indifferent to an observer's approach, big ones and little ones lying in plain sight and ignoring the lures that hopeful fishermen put in front of them. There may be a half dozen big ones that got to be big by slipping into the dark hole of a beaver burrow whenever a human head appeared at the edge of the pond.

In the shallows of the impounded water, a great blue heron may stand, and the mud may show tracks of mink, coyote, black bear, porcupine, deer, moose, or of whatever lesser creatures visit marsh edges high up, to eat, drink, wash, or play. In places, the water shrews dive, swim, or run over the surface like furry water insects. In those mountain wildernesses that are the more inaccessible to man, grizzly bears leave their prints in the game trails skirting the wet shores.

•   •   •

On the high plateaus, near and above timberline, at about eleven thousand feet, there may still be much water: pools and small lakes and glacial flows with some aquatic vegetation. The chief marsh plants above the water are likely to be sedges. Superficially, some of these bodies of water look like lowland pasture sloughs with rather sparse sedgy growths over the shallows and meadows. But here, the frequent violent winds may keep even the sedges washed away in all except sheltered waters.

I spent parts of several summers on an area of four townships of land surrounding the Beartooth Plateau of south-central Montana, studying extremes of range occupied by the muskrats and trying to learn how diminishing habitability for this species grades off into complete uninhabitability at high altitudes, how *any* muskrats *ever* reach the plateau waters on the rare occasions that they do. Fair populations (for mountainous and foothill regions) maintain themselves the year around at less than seven thousand feet on all sides of the plateau; at nine thousand feet, the animals thin out to the extent that they are barely present as *bona fide* residents, and, in some years, they are absent from places formerly occupied.

It is understandable how overflow muskrats from the lower altitudes—if these have enough animals to overflow—could head upstream toward the inhospitable plateau in the same way that muskrats overflowing from Malheur Lake head into the desert; but, on three of four sides of the plateau, precipitous falls and gorges and swift waters are impassable barriers for muskrats trying to work upward. On the fourth side, that nearest Yellowstone Park, where a permanent reservoir of muskrats exists along certain streams, there is a place above the headwaters of one stream where muskrats could cross a relatively few miles of not-too-rough ground and find themselves in waters of the Beartooth Plateau. Pioneering muskrats repeatedly expand the local ranges of the species in summer and early fall, only to have those ranges cut back again by the unendurable conditions imposed by nine months of alpine winter.

There are some marsh creatures about the plateaus. Mink tracks are to be seen in the shore mud, and a moose—a marsh and bog species of northern wilderness—may leave its "sign" among the midsummer snowdrifts. The waters have their own insect life, together with birds to feed upon it. I have seen ducks away up high: a western species of goldeneye and the white-winged scoter. Coyotes and ravens and other enterprising flesh-eaters frequent the high waters. But, as we pass timberline, we find the marshes becoming more and more impoverished and ceasing to be marshes. We still have beauty and pure air and wondrous solitude, but, in a book on marshes, we come to where we no longer belong.

The ecological equivalents of high altitudes are to be seen northward toward the arctic. I have never been farther north than the edge of the subarctic, but many of my friends have. They tell of ponds amid settings of nearly bare rock that must be quite similar to those occurring above timberline in the West. When someone mentions marsh-type vegetation over the tundra ponds, it is—as for the waters of the higher plateaus—likely to be a sedge. Similarities in types of bog plants may be noted at both high altitudes and high latitudes, as in the willows and heaths. However, there are also many differences in classification details even among the more closely related of the arctic-alpine groups of plants.

After all, the differences as well as the similarities between western plateaus and northern tundras have their impacts upon the life that can be maintained on plateau or tundra. The intensity and duration of sunlight and warmth differ much with altitude and latitude during the summer. The western high plateaus always retain much of their winter's chill in the shade, and the shortest nights of midsummer are still long compared with the sunlit summer nights of the North.

• • •

Whether one regards the southern Prairie Provinces as being a geographical extension of the Dakotas or the Dakotas as an extension of the Provinces, similarities in landscape and marshy types should surprise no one.

The Saskatchewan River Delta of central Saskatchewan and Manitoba encompasses millions of acres, in which it is hard to see the lines of demarcation between the delta itself and the greater millions of acres of surrounding wetlands. Stream oxbows lie in marshy or lake-like crescents or in fragments of crescents or in straight channels. To the sides of the river banks lie bogs, swamps, marshes, and lakes. Water can go so many places, and take so long to arrive, that flood water from the spring may still be raising the levels of outlying bodies by early autumn. Ultimately, besides evaporating, some of this water flows across to Hudson Bay, but much just spreads around and settles down in the natural depressions awaiting it over an area that is so vast as to be almost beyond imagination.

Amid the panorama of the ponds and big and little lakes and the spruce and tamarack and willow swamps and the boggy lands between, the Saskatchewan Delta marshes have their cattails, bulrushes, reeds, arrowheads, pondweeds, and waterlilies, as do the marshes of the Dakotas. The northern marshes have local abundances of a scouring rush, which may grow in massed stands, like peculiarly green bulrushes out in the water. The North is further reflected by the moose, woodland caribou, wolves, and Indians, by Hudson's Bay Company and governmental establishments, by sledge

of marshes and marshes 79

dogs kept where people need them, by pontoon planes, and by other manifestations of wilderness and frontier.

I have seen in the Saskatchewan River Delta the same species of ducks that breed on Dakota marshes, though in lesser numbers. Whatever the explanation, be it lack of balanced environment or the failure of local nesting traditions to be maintained, the areas that I visited in what were reputed to be strong wilderness breeding grounds for game ducks in Saskatchewan and Manitoba did not have the ducks that I expected to see.

These mid-north marshes may lack much in fertility, and it is probably no coincidence that the best waterfowl breeding grounds there include the rich delta deposits that new generations of human homeseekers want to drain. It is true that certain forms of animal life abound in places away from the deltas. Marshes and open waters are full of northern pike and sometimes of other fishes, even supporting commercial fisheries. There are famous muskrat and mink marshes. But it is easy to think of a kind of emptiness when traveling over large tracts of this country. It is easy to think that the land is both too old and too young—too old in having had its rocky surface planed away by repeated glaciation—too young in that the last glacial ice withdrew too recently to permit formation of much new soil even where conditions are favorable for soil formation.

Eastward, the marshes in the Precambrian Shield are often small, along sluggish stretches of rivers or in between the lakes. The larger lakes have marshy shallows in many places around the edges, and whole bays may be grown to wild rice or bulrushes. The waters include creeks and rivers that are as swift and cascade-filled as any mountain stream could be and river valleys that are no more than lake chains, whether they constrict to the width of a brook running between hills or are spread out, miles wide, and without perceptible currents. Steep rock faces and wooded islands and surrounding lands covered by coniferous or mixed woods are of this wilderness of the North. It is a land of moose and white-tailed deer in the places suited to these species, of those prize fur-bearers, the marten and the fisher, of mink and otter and red fox and timber wolf.

It is a land of long, cold winters, of deep snow, of quiet air in the depths of spruce and cedar swamps and upland forests. When deep snow restricts the food supply of deer or small owl or fox or seed-eating bird, grouse may still eat aspen buds, snowshoe hares

may still get around in food-rich thickets, red squirrels and chickadees and Canada jays may still thrive in the higher branches
of the trees. Under the snow, as under the ice, a distinctive little
world exists, having its own foods and feeders: the insects and seeds
and green plants, the shrews and mice, the weasels that come down
from above. The winter Northland becomes apportioned into
what is hard or soft, what is confining or spacious, what is cold,
not-so-cold, or warm, what is edible, partly edible, or inedible.

Muskrats live precariously along the shores of open water lakes
or comfortably in the better marshes. They winter with fair security
under the snow-protected cattail shallows—honeycombing the snow
with tunnels, building nests out of the drier vegetation, digging,
gnawing, eating, spending their time staying alive. They live in
the snow-covered peat bogs or on shore somewhat as do their
relatives, the meadow mice, at the same times that meadow mice
may be living out in the marsh in muskrat lodges, somewhat as
do their relatives, the muskrats. Beavers take up residence in marshes
as well as in the more usual places along streams or lake shores;
in marshes, they live much as muskrats do, at times far out from
shore in lodges that look like huge muskrat lodges except that they
contain more and bigger sticks mixed with building material of
cattail and bulrush and waterlily. Again, we have refinements in

artificial classifications not counting too much for animals living or trying to live.

· · · ·

A great deal of what is called the prairie pothole country of southwestern Canada consists of wheat fields spotted with small marshes having the main pattern of open water centers, rush-rimmed shallows, and, on the drier land, encircling aspens. This pothole country—with or without the aspens—is duck country. It is among the best on the continent, though the earlier nests may be buried in snowdrifts and lost, and droughts may entrap flightless ducks of all ages.

The pothole ducks are the pintails, shovelers, teals, gadwalls, and baldpates nesting on dry land, the redheads, canvasbacks, and ruddies nesting over the water in the bulrush cover, and the mallards, bluebills, and ringnecks nesting either on land or over water, as on muskrat lodges. Coyotes and skunks hunt down to the edges of the potholes, and crows search the whole area from above. It is also a land of the heavy-bodied Swainson's hawks, the rangy marsh hawks, and the small sparrow hawks, all hunting in their own ways for the prey they are adapted to take. The larger or more permanent bodies of water have their fish populations, their muskrats and minks, their cormorants, their big loon-like Holboell's grebes along with western and pied-billed grebes, their gulls and terns, their shore birds on mud flats. As fall comes on, so come the northern migrants, from small birds to geese and rough-legged hawks, sometimes snowy owls, and sometimes a wolf from the "bush."

· · ·

Glacial Lake Agassiz once covered an area greater than that of the present Great Lakes combined. Of its marshy remnants, we have the Delta and Netley marshes lying south of Lakes Manitoba and Winnipeg, respectively, Mud and Thief Lakes in northwestern Minnesota, and marshes bordering sluggish streams in the Red River Valley.

At Delta, the marshes vary from thin strips in troughs between ice ridges to wide outlying wetlands that meet the pastures and wheat farms of the slightly higher land. The old ice ridges and beaches between lake and marsh are dominated by such woods and brush as boxelder, ash, pincherry, willow, and poison ivy; the marshes, by reed, cattail, and bulrush. Populations of minks and muskrats vary with the year, the muskrats on occasion suffering heavy mortality from disease and winter freeze-outs. The sand beaches and the meadows are among the skunkiest places that I ever saw. In recent years, a pioneering population of raccoons has appeared. Wetlands, in combination with lake-edge hardwood fringes, provide a focal point for many land as well as water birds.

The Netley marshes differ from those at Delta chiefly because the delta of the Red River is superimposed upon the lake-edge shallows. The northward flow of this stream keeps channels open into Lake Winnipeg, and, when a strong north wind blows, the water piles up at the south end of the lake and pours back through the river channels into the marshes. These wind tides cause fluctuations in water levels of as much as four feet in parts of the marsh near the channels, and fluctuations of decreasing amplitude may be seen many miles from the channels. Wind tides coming during the breeding seasons of marsh life may cause severe losses of nests and young. Muskrat burrows in the low banks may then be flooded, or lodges may separate from the bottom to float wherever wind and waters take them.

When freeze-up on the Netley comes with a storm, an ice-sheet may cover the whole marsh at high water, to be left partially suspended as a brittle seal over banks and the stronger vegetation as the water subsides beneath. As the water continues to go down, new layers of ice form under the outer crust. The surviving muskrats build nests and chambers, plug openings, and run along passageways in the ice and frost, in the partly wet and partly frozen mud and vegetation. In the spring, as the melt waters from the Red River meet still-frozen Lake Winnipeg, there can be further flooding in a period of neither winter nor not-winter. Two such crises— one in fall and the other in the following spring—were estimated by Canadian biologists to have evicted a total of at least fifty thousand muskrats, and the main route of travel of these animals could be traced for about forty miles.

I think of the Netley as a frontier for marsh animals like muskrats. Usually rich in choice foods, it is also large enough and has the right depths of water to support tremendous populations. Yet I do not know if it is ever populated by muskrats up to what might be called full capacity. The wind tides, if not the river floods, are too much to permit security even as muskrats know security.

In addition, there always seems to be some dying from disease, and tracts offering the safer refuge from the wind tides may not have muskrats long remaining alive in them, anyway. Between crises, the muskrats may live well. They are not creatures to worry.

The remnant of glacial Lake Agassiz that I know best is northern Minnesota's Upper Red Lake and parts of the Big Bog extending northward and northeastward from it. The lake is big and often so shallow that a man can walk a half mile out from shore and still not be in water more than waist deep—unless he is on the windward side on a windy day, in which case he can have waves breaking over his head and then water dropping below his knees. Scattered bulrushes somehow maintain themselves out from the wave-swept shores. In the sheltered places, rather dense fringes of bulrushes and reeds with an occasional muskrat lodge in them are marshlike. However, the marshy fringes have their deceptive aspects of habitability for marsh life, for the ice freezes to a depth of four feet or more, deep into the bottom sand; and, when the midwinter push from the square miles of ice-field out on the lake leaves buckled ridges like a continuous row of icy and sandy quonset huts along a shore line, the life that can neither get out of the way nor adjust to the changes is not apt to continue living for long.

The Big Bog—hundreds of thousands of acres—is now mostly an expanse of sphagnum moss, heath, and dead or unthrifty tamaracks. Away from the localized roads and summer cottages, it looks like the wilderness wet lands of the Saskatchewan River Delta. It was the last place to have free-living woodland caribou in the United States—a remnant of a wilderness species living in a remnant of its geographic range. It has the moose and the wolves for which it is well suited. An otter may work a stream, or, in a remote place, a fisher may leave its bounding trail across the snow. Here and there are marshy spots in the Big Bog—a spring flow or a peat burn or a beaver-dammed ditch or a little flow that an ice ridge cut off from the lake.

Whatever may make the differences in terms of excellent range or of marginal range for this or that species, in terms of emergencies or ease of living, the life of the Big Bog is still governed by the laws of life that hold wherever plants and animals live or try to live. As at Bear River, Harney Lake, the Netley marshes, or Wakulla Springs, all in life's responses, or in individual or collective fates of organisms, must be conditioned by what is possible.

7. *of marshes and islands*

Marsh islands of the northern states and northward are often distinctive land areas, partaking of the wildness of the marsh itself. If sufficiently inaccessible, they are as nearly unvisited by man and by man's domestic stock as any of the higher ground about a marsh or lake that we may expect to find in long-settled human communities.

Heavy growths of certain weeds of cultivation may at times take over parts of these island areas having soil that is frequently disturbed, as by ice, wave-action, or rodents. Marsh islands may have their timber cut and be more or less littered with trash and may have shacks or cottages built on them. Still, they are not apt to be put under cultivation, and many of them are man-free for months or even years at a time, except perhaps during the hunting and trapping seasons.

In spring and summer, marsh islands are often the retreats of concentrations of wildlife finding undisturbed breeding conditions when they need them most. This is not to say that the crowded occupants of island breeding grounds live with idyllic security just because they are relieved from human intrusions—though relief from the latter *can* be among the greater blessings that wild things enjoy!

The laws of life may apply to the island-dwellers even more conspicuously than to the dwellers of the real marsh, because of the even greater crowding that may take place on the islands. There is friction between crowded individuals, there is exploitation of the exploitable, and there is death on the islands, but, with man largely out of the scene, the processes of living and dying have the sanction of timeless Order. Of course, modern man is of Life, also, yet his dominance and his faculties for upsetting so much of the rest of life serve to rule him out of what we think of as "natural" relationships of living things.

There could hardly be, it is true, human dominance more complete in its way than the dominance of some islands by fish-eating birds. A small island may have almost nothing alive on it except cormorants and the scavengers, predators, and parasites associated with cormorants and their foods. The cormorant islands reek of dead fish, of excrement, and of combinations of odors unpleasant to the human nose. The ground has its dead birds in all stages of decay and dismemberment, together with the fish bones and the whitewash over all. Similar domination by one or a few species is to be found on island rookeries of pelicans, gulls, and other kinds of colony-nesters.

I am not saying that one must be able to enjoy close contacts with some of these rookeries to appreciate their meaning as natural phenomena, to appreciate their manifestations of life in, yes, its beauteous aspects. For the foulness, by human standards, of the rookeries need not detract from the grace of gulls in flight nor of cormorants in the water, nor from the spectacle—at a distance, if one prefers—of living creatures living as their kinds lived on islands in the ancient seas, lakes, and marshes. We need not impute conscious dignity to wild animals because they look dignified (when they are not squabbling or trying to choke down something too big to swallow), but theirs is still the dignity of the millions of years that they and their behavior patterns have persisted.

Island rookeries are not always dominated by single species to the exclusion of a varied fauna. I have seen many heron rookeries having hundreds of nests concentrated on island areas of a few acres. While it was plain that the herons were there, at least some of these islands were rich in other life. Away from the groups of trees that were loaded with heron nests lived many of the usual animals of islands. Beneath the heron nests would be hunting grounds for predators and scavengers, and a windstorm violent enough to blow nests out of trees might really bring down some exploitable food resources.

One central Iowa island of not much more than an acre had during a single breeding season a rookery of black-crowned night herons, a pair of great horned owls, a mother mink and her family of young, one or two raccoons, a lone fox squirrel, a considerable number of woodchucks, a population of wood mice and cottontails, and, in the bank burrows of the island and of a smaller island adjacent to it, nineteen family groups of muskrats. The plant-eaters found what they needed in the island growths, the herons ate fish, frogs, and invertebrates, the horned owls raided the heron rookery but subsisted chiefly upon prey from the mainland, the raccoons and minks lived upon crayfishes of the shallows. The minks also exploited the young muskrats forced ashore by the population tensions of overproduction. In addition, the island was a favorite loafing ground for pheasants and had attractions for crows and wood ducks. The burrow systems of the dense population of musk-rats thoroughly undermined the banks in places, and the upper parts of the muskrat burrows were used by minks, raccoons, woodchucks, and cottontails. The woodchucks dug right into the chambers of some of the muskrat burrows.

The time came when the herons no longer returned to the island to nest, but that apparently made little difference to the other vertebrates of the island. The island continued to have its pair of horned owls, though these always seemed to be unsuccess-ful in their breeding. The pheasants always showed partiality for it and so did the minks, and it might have a covey of quail or a visiting deer or a red fox from shore, some hundred and fifty yards away. It had the downy woodpeckers and nuthatches and chickadees and brown creepers of woodlands. Its horned owls and minks fed upon the water birds of spring and fall flights. Its dead stubs afforded perches for the rare peregrine falcon or osprey.

I camped on the island the afternoon and night before the duck hunting season opened that year when there was such a concentra-tion of muskrats in the island burrows. High water had killed the cattails, and the stubble of last year's growths stretched out across the open water in almost all directions from the island. In late afternoon, ducks were everywhere on the duckweed-covered water: the not-too-trusting mallards and pintails and the thousands of blue-winged teal, feeding, tipping in the shallows, sitting in bunches, exercising their wings, and losing themselves to sight in shadows and hummocks and dead vegetation. Muskrat wakes broke quiet surfaces, some close by, some so far away that they resembled but moving lines. As light smoke from the supper fire spread out over the water from one side of the island and the haze of evening came on, more muskrat wakes appeared, and the animals lay and sat amid the duckweeds and pondweeds. They ate on the few remaining live cattails and bulrushes and foraged in the shore zones. I counted between forty-five and fifty simultaneously using a hundred yards of shore, while more walked or ran with hunched bodies in the background of sloping shores and abrupt banks. Somewhere would be one bounding along a trail toward the water, vegetation protruding from its mouth and dragging on the ground.

When the night grew chilly, I pulled another thickness of heavy blanket around me. I could not see much over the water, but hoots of horned owls and the clear quacking of mallards carried through the general anonymity of night sounds.

For two or three winters, I jumped a red fox with some regularity during my visits to this island. From the fidelity that it showed toward the same escape routes—the routes used depending upon the direction of my approach over the ice—I suspected that I was observing the behavior of an individual fox. Then, on a fall day before freeze-up, I prowled the edge of the island hunting ducks, and there a fox similar in appearance to the one I had been jumping stood looking at me from a chokecherry thicket about fifteen yards away. It disappeared in the thicket, but, when I got around to the opposite side of the island, it ran out of a gully, stopped on the bank, and turned to watch me, though nearer than before and standing wholly in the open. We looked at each other for about a minute, until the fox slipped along the ridge of the bank into the brush again. I wondered if that island fox might not have come, in the course of my repeated visits without overt acts, to recognize my scent as that of a harmless animal, the shotgun in my hand notwithstanding.

In the following spring, a litter of fox pups was born in a rehabilitated woodchuck hole about in the center of the favorite winter fox retreat. The teething pups came out and chewed on the chokecherry stems around the den entrances and cleaned up the prey remnants to the extent that scarcely anything was left in sight but coot and blackbird wing feathers and a cottontail foot. The island itself offered limited feeding opportunities for a hungry fox family that spring, and, for some weeks, I could not see where the food was coming from, even in the minimal quantities that the pups apparently were getting. The "sign" that gradually took form with the progress of summer was of a fox-scented trail leading from the island's brush down through the fringe of cattails and bulrushes, a watery trail straight across a hundred yards of duckweed-covered bay, to another trail through cattails and bulrushes leading up to the mainland. Any foxes crossing from mainland to island had to swim part of the distance, carrying prey or not, and I am sure that foxes have had easier ways of life. Still, the mainland dogs did not get out to the island dens, the little foxes grew to be big foxes, and my snooping about holes and trails seemed to occasion no worry.

I remember once when my presence on the island was taken more seriously. The surrounding shallows were drought-exposed, and I saw a big old raccoon digging crayfishes out of the mud of an open space. I was about eighty yards from the raccoon on a windy day and intentionally moved to an upwind position to see if the raccoon would catch my scent at that distance. It reared up in my direction, wheeled, and bounded off toward the mainland as fast as if I had shot at it.

So far as a dominant form of life on this island is concerned, neither the herons of years ago nor the enterprising flesh-eaters that lived with and followed them quite seem to fit the role. The herons did not make out as permanent residents, though I do not know why not. The horned owls were permanent residents but their reproductive failures illustrate the marginality of this island environment for them as a species; as adult birds, they thrive there, and I can visualize the place as always having its horned owls, as being the sort of place to attract new owls each year if something tragic befalls the old residents. Yet, it lacks the nesting facilities to perpetuate its own horned owl population—it has no hollow trees large enough for horned owl nests. Lacking hollow trees, the owls need nests of red-tailed hawks or crows for their own nesting, and the redtails and crows of the neighborhood will not nest on such a small island as long as the owls are so much on the scene, and the owls are always somewhere around.

The raccoons and foxes can be prominent parts of the island's life, and so can a white-tailed deer when it tramples snow and browses in a sheltered corner. So can the minks when they take over muskrat burrows and leave muddy tracks about holes in snow and ice, crisscross new and old snow with trails, and drag over to the island the bodies of waterfowl and muskrats from anywhere on the marsh. So can the muskrats when the periphery of the island becomes almost a continuous set of burrows. Despite everything predatory, any winter snow that has lain on the island overnight in condition to take and keep tracks may be expected to have cottontail tracks. But no one of these species so much characterizes the life of this particular island in my mind as do the woodchucks.

Woodchuck holes occur both on top of and along the sides of the island, from the highest points down to the water's edge, under root tangles of trees, in thickets, in nettle patches, under glacial rocks, and on open ground. The burrows are newly dug, they are weathered, they are rehabilitated old burrows, they have brittle woodchuck bones in their earth heaps—and muskrat and rabbit bones, or maybe raccoon or skunk bones. I never could make satisfactory estimates of the island's woodchuck population at any one time, nor even judge whether the diggings and trails were of one or more family groups—there are often heavily-used, interconnecting overland trails between main burrow systems. I do know that young chucks are raised there, and probably some surplus young go to the mainland. Passage of woodchucks to and from the mainland occurs, during both drought exposures of the shallows and periods of high water.

●　　●　　●　　●

A little island on the home farm in South Dakota had its numerous muskrat burrows, its minks, and, whenever it had land connections, its visiting skunks. Its trees had the small tree birds of lake shores and the herons and the kingfishers. Instead of a population of woodchucks to burrow the higher ground, it had a population of Franklin's ground-squirrels ("gray gophers"). Its ground-squirrels, like the woodchucks of the central Iowa island, were not marooned from the adjacent mainland any more than they wanted to be, either at times of high water or low. They left tracks on the sand or drying mud of exposed land connections, along with the skunk tracks and mink tracks and heron tracks and shore bird tracks; and I did not consider it an astounding sight to see ground-squirrels swimming.

The home farm island has many memories for me as a camp site, and I do not forget, either, how often I would go out of my way just to visit it, to see what was new and interesting, if not profitable from a predatory standpoint. The memories of herons squawking overhead in the night and ground-squirrels whistling during the day while I fished for bullheads from the bank are all in the picture, and so is a memory of a week-end, planned for duck hunting, but spent instead in the dripping gloom of a tent during an almost constant downpour. What I remember still more, when I really think of the island, are the little scenes from brief visits: the tracks of crows, muskrats, mallards, and minks in wet slush, the mink tracks in snow almost everywhere, leading to old ground-squirrel holes, into snowdrifts, under gooseberry bushes, across open spaces, the bloody holes in the ice and the clam shells over muskrat channels, the fresh bubbles and food remains floating under new ice. A freeze-up caught our flock of about a dozen Pekin ducks across the lake from the farmyard, and, while the ducks were waddling on the ice, the minks killed every one of them and dragged the bodies into holes, mostly into holes on the island. That gave the island a special attractiveness for minks for some weeks thereafter.

The droughts of the mid-thirties killed the island's trees and transformed it into a mainland hill, whereupon it became covered with buckbrush, and the mallards took it over for nesting. After the water came back, muskrats again lived in bank burrows, and minks again worked the edges. The island again had integrity as a wild island, but some of the terms in its biotic equation had changed. Two decades after the great droughts, a few small hardwood trees were rising above the buckbrush.

• • •

I know several islands in northern Iowa marshes offering a wide variety of ecological conditions. These have their higher ground partly covered with big trees and their lower ground with a brushy, grassy fringe grading off into wet meadow. The more extensive or interconnected island groups have essentially their own animal life. Fox squirrels, horned and screech owls, woodpeckers, and the common woodland songbirds nest in the trees, shrikes and brown thrashers nest in the plum thickets, and tree swallows nest in the dead willow fringes. Raccoons, red foxes, skunks, minks, weasels, ground-squirrels, meadow mice, deer mice, shrews, woodchucks, meadowlarks, ducks, and garter snakes occur on either the higher ground or the low ground. Near the meadow's edge live the rails, blackbirds, muskrats, and crayfishes. The trails of eaters and eaten lead in and out of the water and everywhere in between. The low grassy or brushy islands can be among the most life-rich of the northern prairies and on which duck nests may be concentrated by the dozens or even by the hundreds. About these islands one may hear the whinnying of sora rails and the calling of frogs and toads.

• • • •

Low-lying peninsulas may also have wildlife populations similar to those of the islands. The area having the most consistently high populations of breeding waterfowl, minks, and island-type life of which I know in northern Iowa is a sprawling, irregular series of peninsular meadows indented by shallow bays. It is so inconveniently accessible to motorized man as to have—with respect to human disturbance—many of the advantages of the less accessible of marsh islands. It is in the middle of a four-section tract of land, where geese loiter during migration and where willets and other big or rare shore birds are apt to appear if they appear at all in that part of the state.

Separate mink families may live on almost every peninsula. Raccoons, skunks, foxes, opossums, crows, gulls, terns, kingfishers, marsh hawks, and herons work the meadows and uplands that they find profitable working; and the local crayfishes are staple diet for all of these except when something else happens to be more available.

It is rather plain that the advantages that isolation offers to island-dwelling forms are advantages only of degree. Seldom does the isolation of an island give anywhere nearly complete protection to anything. The minks having their young on islands stand a better chance of rearing them without molestation by dogs, foxes, or coyotes, but both wild and tame dogs may reach the marsh islands. Even if they do not, there can be killing of minks by minks as crowding becomes pronounced. The island-nesting birds suffer a certain amount of loss from the minks and other mammalian predators that are already there, and it takes real isolation to be valid against the predators that fly. Even the great rookeries of island-nesting birds may be vulnerable to raiding by crows, ravens, and gulls in the absence of predatory mammals. However, absence of members of the weasel and dog families on islands may encourage some of the greater concentrations of the ground-nesting birds. But then, if a mink or a fox or a coyote ever does get over, the status of the concentrated island-nesters may be worse than on the mainland.

We need not assume that the island-dwellers are uniformly helpless against those racial enemies by which they are frequently visited. Some—such as the larger herons and geese—can be dangerous for ordinary predators of mink or fox or raccoon sizes to molest. Less formidable defenders may still be capable of more mobbing power than predators care to invite. Moreover, the individual birds or groups of birds among the colony-nesters show much variation in their own security or breeding success. One trend of the evidence coming out of wildlife investigations is that predation is largely centered on the parts of populations having the poorer places in which to live or on the parts of populations having trouble with their own kind. What goes on in natural relationships on marsh islands is much in keeping with the evolution of the participants, of the eaters or the eaten.

We come back to the idea of islands being among the better places for wildlife if only to the extent that they may keep man away during some of the critical months of each year. I have known marsh islands in Iowa and South Dakota that were covered by growths of poison ivy entirely sufficient to discourage people from wading or rowing out to them, to mess around irresponsibly among the duck

nests. In the Precambrian Shield, many islands are bounded by such sheer rock faces that only people having mountaineering ability ever climb up on them. These are retreats of species that particularly do want to be left alone, such as peregrines or eagles nesting far above the water. The rough country north of Lake Superior has islands so high and so precipitous that they resemble great pillars.

Some areas in the Precambrian Shield have islands nearly everywhere in wilderness lake chains, well away from places where people go, away from the can-littered canoe routes. They may be barren islands or partly wooded or heavily wooded, left to the mergansers and goldeneyes and whatever else there is to fly, swim, or wade out to them. Islands may lie near the mainland or be connected with it by rocky or sandy shallows or by a continuation of marshy fringes or by bogs or willow swamps. Islands may grade into peninsulas. There may be a moose in the lily pads, a bear in the blueberries, red squirrels in the pines, a beaver lodge on one side and deep water on another. On islands or on peninsulas, the minor distinctions between them are ignored by the creatures finding them accessible and livable.

• • •

Although the rock islands of the Precambrian Shield may be thought of as being almost as permanent as the earth—composed as they are of some of earth's oldest rocks—the islands of glacial debris are likely to persist only until the next glaciation. Many of the latter have had the time to realize most of their possibilities as living places for island species of plants and animals. The islands of modern deltas and stream channels, in contrast, sometimes do not last long.

On the wind- and stream-flooded Netley marshes south of Lake Winnipeg, the higher and more permanent of the islands offer refuge to marooned mammals during high water. They have their deer and coyotes, their mice and minks, and prey and predators live close together when the waters force withdrawals from the surrounding lowlands. Life may then become a matter of finding the safest hummock or tree crotch or unsubmerged hole and waiting out the flood.

Along the lower bank islands bordering the central channels, the muskrats stay as long as they can as the water rises in their burrows, and they open up the tops and enlarge the chambers just below the surface of the ground. As the water nears the top or covers the ground, they must come out, to build nests anchored in whatever vegetation there is along the banks or out in the marsh, or to sit in the scrub willows, or to lie quietly, trying to remain in the neighborhood, somehow. If there are helpless young in the banks, the mother may deposit them, one by one, all or only part of the litter, in a drier place outside. Young of swimming sizes may lie in a pile in the water, in a hole or in a nest, the lower ones withdrawing to climb on the others, until some become too weak to withdraw any more, and their bodies lie, a platform of dead young flesh supporting the still-living young flesh. At high flood, all the muskrats of the low bank islands may be gone, the old and the young and their nests and sitting places. Dead and living bodies may float away, toward the lake along the flowing channels or off somewhere across the marsh, over the channels and banks and washed down vegetation.

The channel islands themselves come and go in consequence of wave washings, the action of ice, or changes in flow of streams. Mud- or sandbars remaining until annual plants have a chance to colonize them are not unused by wildlife and may often show areas of new plant growths fed upon by muskrats, beavers, and waterfowl. If they last a few years longer as islands, they may be covered by grasses and sedges, by saplings of ash, willow, cottonwood, and similar stream-edge hardwoods. Old channel islands have old forest on them but their relative impermanence is still betrayed by the undercutting of the big trees by the current in one place, together with the building of new bars in another.

•   •   •

Dense stands of aquatic plants separate from the bottom muck and rise up to form another type of island. Floating cattail islands support in their dry and tangled upper parts not only the muskrat lodges and nests that one expects to find in cattails but also populations of garter snakes, mice, and nesting birds, and sometimes even such dry land animals as striped ground-squirrels. These islands are most conspicuous on some marshes that are about to become open water lakes and may represent virtually all of the broad-leaved cattails able to stay alive after the dying of the stands remaining rooted to the bottom.

The muskrat lodges may themselves be islands, having their own insects, spiders, snakes, turtles, bird nests, toads, mice. Meadow mice live in and about some of these lodges much as the muskrats do, swimming, climbing, and, if pursued, diving. Such mouse populations are truly of the marsh, the year around, reproducing their kind over the water, feeding on exposed rootstocks of bulrushes or on the summer greenery. It is tempting to conjecture how muskrats came to be muskrats in the course of geologic time, insofar as they are, in skeletal structure, but overgrown meadow mice. The meadow mice have a good start on the adaptations of muskrats.

•   •   •

When I lived on the old home farm amid the lakes and marshes of east-central South Dakota, a place known as the "Goodfellow island" was a peninsula rather than an island. It was a tract of a hundred acres of pasture, with little marshes between hills and a big marsh bounding one of its four sides. Open-water lakes having reedy or rushy coves bounded the other three sides. (When the water first came back after the droughts of the mid-thirties, this "island" was almost surrounded by marshy waters, but that does not represent its usual state.) The neck of land that made it a peninsula lay at one corner of our farm, and, as the pasture was owned and used by a jovial neighbor, it was always within my regular home range for prowling, hunting, and trapping.

The "Goodfellow island," not being at all conveniently near the owner's buildings on the far side of one of the lakes, usually had in it only livestock requiring a minimum of care. Often, I must have been the only person to be on it for weeks at a time. It was one of the places where coyotes could still live in some safety during years when they were all but hunted out over the whole county. Except at the boundary of an alfalfa field on our land, most wildlife there had little more access to the products of human agriculture than they must have had during the days of the Indians and the bison. The bark-fed cottontails sat in primeval innocence in the lake shore thickets and let me pick them off one by one with any firearm that I might have along. Not so independent of man were the prairie chickens that boomed on the hills in the spring and roosted in the slough grass in winter. They required a proper ecological balance of undisturbed wildness and such blessings of cultivation as the corn and small grains that a farm could provide.

Muskrats usually thrived in the deeper bulrush and cattail marshes of the hills during the breeding season, along with the minks and ducks and blackbirds. The shallower of the marshes tended to go dry in late summer, which was all right for the minks, ducks, and blackbirds but not so advantageous or even endurable for the muskrats. The latter could find themselves in trouble before midwinter. They gnawed holes out through frozen bank burrows or the sides of lodges, fed upon debris of dry plant stems or upon the few rootstocks or tubers of marsh plants that they could reach from above. I dug out nests in snowdrifts and followed trails in snow, trails along the lake shore from one ice-heave to another. Victims finally died of fight-wounds, hunger, and cold, were eaten by other desperate muskrats or by minks or mice or crows, or lay sodden and exposed to view by the spring thaws.

Besides the minks, the place had a regular predatory fauna of weasels and badgers and many striped skunks. The staple foods of these were characteristic of both uplands and lowlands of east-central South Dakota: the rabbits, mice, and ground-squirrels, the beetles and grasshoppers and water insects of grasslands and marshes, the crayfishes and frogs and snakes, and the fishes of the surrounding lakes.

With or without man, the "Goodfellow island" was a natural sanctuary for native wildlife. Everything seemed fitting for a naturally self-sustaining combination of animal communities and everything seemed to fit. The colonies of nesting red-winged black-birds, each with its own territorial subdivisions, the meadowlarks nesting on the hills, the screech owls and the flickers in the lake shore cottonwoods, the pair of marsh hawks, the few pairs of crows, the garter snakes and bull snakes and snapping turtles, all represented animals adjusted to what they had. At times of natural crises, the aquatic life furnished tremendous quantities of food for the creatures able to exploit it, and then many opportunistic hunting and scavenging forms came from surrounding areas. The drying of the big marsh usually bounding one side meant concentrations of herons —not only of night herons from a rookery across the lake but also great blues that seemed to be drawn in from the entire lake chain. The semi-annual bird migrations always meant new food for flesh-eaters, especially in the form of the ailing ducks sitting around at the last of the spring migration and the fall migrants that could not leave at freeze-up.

Storms put much edible matter on the beaches. I often saw in the broken plant debris of beach drift choice fishes that were so clean and fresh that I was tempted to take them home to eat but never quite dared to: walleyes, ten-pound northerns, and big sun-fishes. Just before one freeze-up, a windstorm washed up hundreds of snapping turtles. An old note describes snappers being tossed in the drift at intervals of every five to twenty feet along a six-hundred-yard stretch of rocky shore. The stranded snappers would try to get back into the lake, always, so far as I could see, unsuccessfully. On their sides and backs and in normal positions, those snappers were still there at dusk, when the spray was beginning to freeze, still numbly moving their feet. And there, the freeze-up caught them, and their bodies were iced over, gathered snow, and the snow blew around them, as they lay like so many lake-side rocks. Then, with thawing of their ice and snow covering, they were turtles again, and not rocks, and the winter's hungry flesh-eaters pecked and gnawed and wrenched.

• • •

My memories of the "Goodfellow island" are linked with memories of my personal depredations upon its wildlife because that was the way in which I lived. I remember one quiet June afternoon and evening for the thousands of lake buffalo spawning in the shallows—and for the killing, cleaning, and salting of a barrel of fish—enough to last us well into the summer. Yet, if anything, my memories of some things that did not profit me directly are even stronger, as of spring holes in the ice near shore packed with minnows, perch, and bullheads too small to eat.

I was on the "Goodfellow island" a great deal at night during my trapping years. It was not only on one of the most direct routes home at the end of some of my traplines, and offering passably easy walking, but it also held the allure of the not-quite-to-be-expected. My hopes were always to be able to sneak up on a coyote howling from a hilltop, but nothing like that ever worked out for me. Nevertheless, I would stand a better chance of seeing a weasel or a mink abroad in the night or at least some of the more common-place of night creatures—if nothing more than jackrabbits—disporting themselves a little more openly than during the day. There might be night sounds hinting more of mystery than the daytime sounds. There might be some kind of adventure.

One mild and brightly moonlit night in early December, I was cutting off toward home and saw a huge skunk ambling between the hills—a five-dollar piece of fur in those days. The only firearm that I had with me was a heavy revolver loaded with two cartridges, so I ran after the skunk to try to get in a position for a certain shot. The skunk speeded up and so did I, the back pocket of my hunting coat half full of wet muskrat skins slapping as I ran. As I caught up, the skunk would dodge or threaten to throw scent, then run off again, to dodge some more, never holding still long enough to give me good aim. So, in the December moonlight, we played the old game of predator and prey up and down the hills, until the skunk ran straight ahead and I ran beside it, hip boots pounding the frosty ground. As we ran together about five feet apart and about as fast as we both could go with what we had left, I got off a shot, and the skunk went into a roll of waving tail and feet and black and white limpness. I gave my prey time to die, returned the revolver with its remaining cartridge to the holster, shucked off hunting coat, rolled up shirt sleeves, and got out the skinning knife for one more job under the midnight moon.

•   •   •

I have not been on the "Goodfellow island" for many years. In the mid-fifties, I saw from a distance that, as in other parts of my old farm neighborhood, its hills were plowed and planted to corn. Perhaps, some of its long-undrained marshes have been drained. It still had no buildings, however, and I think that man is unlikely to change it to the extent that it will no longer offer comparatively good environment for native wildlife. Its strategic location and the rough land of its edges assure it of some permanence in that respect. Whether I ever go on it again or not, I am glad that it exists.

I know that some people whom I respect maintain that natural beauties are valueless unless human eyes may be present to appreciate them, and, to such opinions, my only reply is that not all of us feel that way. To me, the fact of being is justification for natural beauties. One who loves the out-of-doors should not necessarily have to visit islands or peninsulas in person to enjoy the thought of their existence. These islands and peninsulas are a delight to me in that they may maintain so much of their wilderness integrity, in that they may be so much a part of naturalness where naturalness belongs.

8. *of marshes and safety and comfort*

As in other places, a person may find a certain range of discomforts and dangers about a marsh if he happens to be unfamiliar with the possibilities.

Without here attempting any complete coverage of the obvious, let me remind the careless hunter that he may injure or kill himself or another in an accident on a marsh as well as on land. I never witnessed a hunting accident and never knew personally anyone who suffered in a serious hunting accident, but I did see about a marsh-edge boat landing the smeared brains and blood of a stranger, which meant that someone would be unlikely to enjoy the thought of that marsh again. Neither is a marsh any place for indiscreet drinking, nor for physical excesses by persons for whom excesses would be dangerous anywhere. Marsh mud *can* be hard wading, and an out-of-condition or an elderly person may undertake more wading than he should. A friend of mine once helped carry out the body of an epileptic hunter who drowned in knee-deep water.

A boat may swamp or upset, but the usual shallowness of marsh water delimits the consequences of such mishaps. Despite the decreased likelihood of outright drownings on a marsh, there may still be the problem of mud if the shore is any considerable distance away.

The mud problem varies with circumstances and with the marsh. Marsh bottoms may be sandy or gravelly or otherwise firm; they may have enough of an underlayer of cattail or bulrush or waterlily rootstocks to give passable footing even over soft bottom; or they may have two or three feet of the soupiest, stickiest, most unwadeable mud. Marshes may be wadeable one year and not so another, depending upon previous drought exposures and action of ice and water.

The potentialities of marsh muds may be learned quite well with experience. Even a novice, by a little testing and observation, soon picks up the essentials for getting along. A canoe paddle or an oar should be carried for testing depths and for steadying oneself whenever much wading needs to be done. Wading, like snowshoeing, calls for the use of muscles that are underdeveloped in the legs of most people. After these muscles become strengthened, wading becomes much easier than before.

Rubber boots and waders, if worn with insufficient padding of socks, rub blisters on heels; and anyone who has reason to fear blisters should not only wear the proper amount and quality of socks but should also protect heels with surgical tape. It may also be suggested that new trousers be well laundered before being worn in sweaty boots, in order to prevent skin eruptions from contact with the chemical irritants often found in garments fresh from dry goods counters. Some veteran marsh men wear tennis shoes and ordinary trousers for wading in warm weather, but prolonged soaking of the skin in certain waters may invite attack by the parasites responsible for "swimmer's itch" or result in other (though usually minor) unpleasantnesses.

Water over a boot top may be a special problem in cold weather. If only a little water spills over—enough to feel but not enough to make one very wet—a person in good health may ignore it until returning home. After a thorough wetting of the lower garments and with no change or heat-drying feasible, the best thing might be to wring out the wet clothes and put them back on. Woolen socks and underwear can be damp and still comfortable if the air temperature is not too low and if the wearer keeps moving.

•　　•　　•

A marsh is a place where it is possible to become thirsty. I found this out repeatedly when I was young, but it was not until well after I attained the legally designated age of discretion that I regularly carried with me a mason jar of drinking water. Marsh water is not necessarily foul nor full of pathogenic microorganisms simply because it may be stagnant, overlying mud, or choked with vegetation. There usually are, however, so many uncertainties about marsh water that the drinking of it unboiled or untreated should be avoided. Of course, when we consider waters with botulism toxin, we get into a special case, but no normal man in circumstances short of desperation should need warnings with the sight and smell of death around him.

The idea that human beings are especially in danger of "catching something" from supposedly pestilential marsh waters or marsh mud in our north-central region is unfortunate. I confess that I do not enjoy working with a die-off of muskrats from their hemorrhagic disease, and that I am afraid of the disease, itself, but that falls in the category of an occupational rather than a public hazard, so far as it is a hazard. The only persons, other than scientists, whom I know to have contracted any disease even from handling great numbers of muskrats in our region were a very few trappers contracting tularemia over a long period of years—at the rate of only one trapper in many, many thousands. I never knew a duck hunter or anyone else to contract any kind of infection from wading with boots or from boating in marsh waters, as such. The odors coming off a marsh in the spring following a winter-kill of fishes may not be inspiring to human noses, but they neither poison nor infect the air.

•   •   •   •

Some infectious diseases *may* be transmitted to man via insect or tick bites, and marshes are among the places where transmission may occur.

"Wood ticks" of marsh borders are carriers of Rocky Mountain spotted fever as well as of tularemia. The abundance and proportions of infective ticks vary locally, but it is well not to let ticks become attached to skin, and to remove carefully (without squeezing bodies) those that do become attached. Some people may work day after day for years around marsh edges and brushy or wooded lowlands in tick season (late spring to midsummer) without having a tick attached. As I write this, the last occurrence that I recall for my own body was more than fifteen years ago. I see the ticks on my khaki trousers or shirts or feel them crawling on my skin before they can fasten on.

Among the widely-held misconceptions concerning mosquitoes and glacial marshes that need straightening up is that the marsh itself must be an uncomfortable place for people to be in summer. Meadows and woods about marshes and, to some extent, the marsh edges may have mosquitoes by the billions, but I have usually found genuine mosquitoes scarce out over the water and amid the bulrushes, cattails, and reeds. I have found this to be true in the north-central region clear up to the subarctic, even in mosquito country that may properly be termed "awful." Contrasts may be sharp in the Canadian North, where one may paddle or ride in mosquito-free peace just about wherever the water floats a canoe, yet run into hungry clouds upon landing.

Malaria does not happen to be in the marsh picture with which I am familiar (although some of our north-central marshes are within the geographic ranges of species of mosquitoes that *could* transmit the parasites of human malaria), but, in some localities in some years, mosquitoes may transmit at least encephalitis. Under extreme conditions, mosquitoes that are innocuous as disease transmitters may be dangerous to man through their mass attacks. None need belittle the power of aggressive mosquitoes to inflict misery.

There are things that can be done to avoid being bitten by mosquitoes—such as restricting outdoor activities to the most mosquito-free times of day and to the most mosquito-free weather, or, conversely, planning to be behind netting during the dark or shady hours or at times when the air lies so still and muggy as to bring out the little bodies wherever they are. But, maybe it is necessary for a person to be among them.

The modern, externally applied mosquito repellents are excellent, having effectiveness lasting up to an hour or longer except when washed rapidly away by perspiration. It probably will not be long until we may buy effective repellents to be taken internally. Repellents do not make mosquitoes enjoyable, for, if attacking in swarms, they may still get in eyes, ears, mouth, and nostrils, even when not biting. Head nets and similar coverings may be preferred by some people, but they can be hot as well as cumbersome to wear.

Again, the problem of mosquitoes is not likely to be serious out on a pleasant north-central glacial marsh, with open water and emergent vegetation and summer breezes. In this region, the mosquitoes are in the grassy and sedgy meadows, in the leatherleaf bogs, in the shrubbery and deep woods, in our backyards and gardens at home, in the lawns where we try to cool off on a summer evening and either do something with DDT or other chemicals or sit there and swat and swat until we give up and go inside.

Marshes may have deer flies or tabanids, mostly the big ones known as "bull dogs" or those a couple of sizes smaller having dark patches on their wings. They may hardly be noticeable, if active at all, or they may be extremely annoying. They are by no means exclusively a marsh pest—when pestiferous about marshes, they may be still more so ashore, in fields, pastures, and about farm-yards. They should not be permitted to bite, for the bites hurt and later itch—sometimes intensely and for days—and a western species is a notorious transmitter of tularemia.

I can remember them as an absolute curse at three places: a northern Iowa marsh, a northern Minnesota marsh, and the earlier-mentioned Locomotive Springs north of Great Salt Lake. They were bad about the Iowa marsh only during part of one summer, and a violent midsummer rainstorm almost eliminated them for the remainder of the season. At the Iowa and Min-nesota marshes, it was the discomfort of being bitten and the neces-sity for constantly fanning them away that made them such a problem; on the Utah desert, they were not only the most persistent and swarming of attackers, but there was also the menace of their tularemia.

The mosquito repellents that I have tried seem only partly efficacious against deer flies, but the presence of some repellents on the skin may prevent actual biting; and some of the pyrethrum preparations sprayed on headgear may discourage these flies from circling around. Unless they are extraordinarily troublesome, I seldom do any more than keep systematically brushing them away

of marshes and safety and comfort   105

from exposed skin surfaces and otherwise avoid giving them opportunities to settle down for a bite.

Similar procedures are usually sufficient against the biting gnats and stable flies that can be so attentive in the north-central region and northward. Of these, again, relatively few may be expected to show up on the marsh itself in comparison to the numbers that may await on land. If the day happens to be the right sort for being bitten and one lacks any repellents that seem to work, substantial protection may be gained simply by wiping by hand, with alternating movements, the sides of neck and face nearest each hand. Such movements may be so systematized that they take hardly any conscious effort when they are needed, coming at natural intervals while wading or walking or between paddle strokes.

At times, marsh insects are a nuisance chiefly in that they fly all around one's head in large numbers. They vary from small gnats to big midges. Often, they make no attempts to alight on skin and, when they do, it may be only incidentally. It is easier to ignore them when it is apparent that they are not biting, or, if it is hard to ignore them, some of the repellents used against the biting flies might be tried.

•   •   •

With respect to bites of a different sort, anyone may be advised *not* to reach without good reason into retreats of muskrats, minks, raccoons, or other hole-dwellers. In connection first with trapping and later with scientific work, I received some severe bites from muskrats and I doubt if anyone would care to have them duplicated for the experience. All of my own bite wounds from muskrats came from either captured animals or mothers defending their young from my intrusions, and thus were not from bites likely to befall just anybody.

The public should also be warned against carelessly approaching muskrats met on land. Such muskrats, in their fear at being away from the safety of water, may quickly turn on anyone moving toward them and, for their size, they can be formidable attackers of legs and whatever other parts of a person's body they can reach.

These seemingly unprovoked attacks by muskrats are a frequent basis for rabies scares. Muskrats are known to contract rabies on rare occasions, but ferocious self-defense is an attribute of the healthy animals. Rabies is, nevertheless, something to watch out for anywhere, in wild and domestic animals alike, in town and about the countryside. Any wild mammal that does not act quite right should be regarded with caution, particularly if it be fox, coyote, raccoon, skunk, or squirrel, and more particularly if it be of any normally wary species that shows singular tameness. In our north-central region, the foxes, raccoons, and skunks may sicken and die from various diseases not considered dangerous to man, but rabies is one of the possibilities that always should be remembered for the sake of personal safety.

Some of the rattlesnakes known as massasaugas live about some north-central wetlands. Farther west, other species of rattlers may occur down to the shore zones of marshes, and I suppose that the timber rattler of the East may now and then visit a marsh edge. To the south, one may find numerous poisonous snakes (notably cotton-mouths and diamondbacks) in wet places. I have never seen any poisonous snake about any marsh from central Iowa northward and northwestward through central and western Minnesota and the eastern Dakotas.

No one should be careless with snapping turtles nor believe the old saying that a snapper will not bite one under water. Seek trouble with a snapper, and it will try to give it to you. A bite by a huge snapper could cut off a hand. But I have never known a snapper to make an unprovoked attack upon a human being, nor have I ever known the common painted turtles or the Blanding's turtles of our marshes to be risky to handle.

• • •

A north-central marsh may be perceptibly cooler than the surrounding land in hot weather. During the hot summers of 1934 and 1936, with recorded air temperatures often exceeding a hundred degrees Fahrenheit for many consecutive days, the northern Iowa marshes were among the places remaining comfortable in the out-of-doors. With breezes and the delicately sweet odors of pond-weed flowers over the water, the occasional designing deer fly could be batted down with good humor.

The possibility of sudden changes in weather should be realistically considered. From hot sunshine to cold rain or hail is not an unheard-of switch in our North American interior, and, if there be danger in a thorough chilling, it can be on a marsh as well as on land. Summertime marsh equipment should therefore include a

raincoat to be grabbed if dark or greenish clouds come rolling along too fast to permit one to reach shore and cover. (Although I was never caught out over water in anything proving to be a dangerous storm, I missed the impact of the most violent rainstorm of my experience by racing to shore and getting under a canoe as a cloudburst struck.)

Hunting season weather calls for still greater care in avoiding serious discomforts and dangers. The "Armistice Day Blizzard" of 1940 killed many hunters marooned on islands or otherwise exposed to the storm. Tragedies and near-tragedies are reported in the newspapers every fall—the hunters in a boat who lost their oars (and had no spares along) and were blown out to the rough open water of a lake to drown, the two old men who went out in a one-man boat that sank and left them standing up to their armpits in icy water until they were rescued in helpless condition—some having

of marshes and safety and comfort

misfortunes due to unluckiness and some to unwisdom. Of lesser seriousness but scarcely conducive to enjoyment are the standard mistakes of the inexperienced. We have the youngster in shirt sleeves a long way from home and the wind getting colder or perhaps snow coming down from the same sky from which the sun's warmth was coming when he set forth. Or the people who have to learn of the limitations of light gloves as covering for hands in freezing weather or of leather shoes and conventional socks as wet-weather foot gear, or anyone who does not know that it may be important to have warm clothes on his chest, whether other body parts feel warm or not.

• • •

In referring to the dangers of ice, I do not mean especially the possibilities of slipping and falling—although I have taken ice-falls so hard that I lay there and groaned until I could get up and move on. If a person keeps control of gun or axe or other dangerous or valuable equipment while falling, and softens and guides the fall by letting knees give way while losing balance, he should be able to take the actual hazard out of nearly all ice-falls. A person experienced in falling may do the proper thing automatically. In my middle age, I fall on ice many times each winter and think little of it.

The dangers of ice that come to my mind are those of ice in combination with water underneath. The ice may be too weak to hold a man's weight yet too strong to wade through or to push through easily with a metal boat or canoe. There are few exercises to compare with trying to walk on ice that holds only until one gets up on it. This sort of thing—to the accompaniment of skinning shins inside of boots and falling down in the water and mud as the ice gives way—may become most tiresome.

Appalling demonstrations of poor judgment may be seen on the part of the hunting public taking chances with ice. One afternoon, when the not-so-thick ice of an Iowa marsh was becoming too soft for safety, a party of hunters walked all around in the central bulrushes where the water in places was so deep that they might well have drowned if they had broken through. Their maneuverings were watched with apprehension and commented upon by several other parties of hunters staying on shore, and one of the local residents kept a telescope on them. Ultimately, the party walked off the lake to their car, a group of young men from a city, some of whom did not even wear boots. They displayed no awareness of having been luckier than anyone expected.

I remember, back in South Dakota, a man who went through the ice and stood with feet on the bottom and little more than his head out of the water. He had to wait there until his rescuers could work out to him with boards from the nearest farmyard. Another man, an Iowan with more modern advantages, walked out on the morning ice of a sealed-over marsh and settled himself on a muskrat lodge, from which position he banged away at high-flying ducks without competition from hunters ashore. He did not drop any ducks and, when ready to come in, discovered that the ice was nothing to walk on. So there he sat and yelled until the town fire department came out and rescued him.

If it is essential to walk on thin or rotten ice, one may at times pick out the safer parts on the basis of color, proximity to vegetation, or some other criteria that might be practical under given circumstances. Few rules may be proposed for doing this, for sometimes it is the dark ice that is stronger and sometimes the lighter. Vegetation may either shade the ice or concentrate the sun's rays upon it, or thicken it by collecting small quantities of snow to melt down partially and then refreeze, or weaken it by collecting sufficient snow to prevent deeper freezing. Firm thin ice is more trustworthy than much thicker ice that is in a honeycomb stage of melting.

Ice may be weakened by the warmth of decomposing plant materials beneath. Parts of a marsh having much decomposition may freeze over lightly or remain open, and these parts must be watched for. So must sites of springs, thin spots over entrances to beaver or muskrat lodges, places where ice-buckling keeps the water more or less open, and the places last to freeze over while the water birds stayed around. The big danger periods are either shortly after freeze-up or during heavy thaws.

Quick action may spare one a thorough wetting. I know how it feels to be left standing with boots full of water, but, many times, when breaking through some concealed soft spot, I kicked my feet and threw myself on solid ice quickly enough to prevent going in over the tops of hip boots. The only dangerous break-through that I ever had was into a thinly frozen, snowed-over hole that ducks had kept open in lake ice. On this occasion, I turned my body around toward the solid ice, slid my gun ahead of me, kicked myself out of the water, and crawled away. It was all done in an instinctive, continuing motion, before getting wet over my hips. I do not know whether I could do it as well another time, nor how much luck another person might have in doing it.

A strong pole is useful both for testing dangerous ice and for support in the event of a break-through. If upright walking is too hazardous (and one is out on the ice and must keep going), it may be possible to crawl. Boards, poles, or skis may also be used to redistribute a person's weight on weak ice. Some hunters and trappers are expert in using light metal boats with sled runners over very weak ice; they can slip in and out of the open spots.

Yes, there are things that can be done on weak ice by those having equipment and know-how, but it should be emphasized that weak ice over dangerous water or mud should be treated respectfully. No one should be encouraged ever to take chances with it unless for the best of reasons, and about the only valid reason of which I can think is to try to help someone who is already in trouble. At any such time, too, it behooves a rescuer to use his head, for a second person in trouble in icy water is not any great help to the first.

Thin or rotten ice may be best enjoyed by human beings from the shore. Watch the ducks alighting in the patches of open water or sitting on the ice that holds them. Watch the muskrats swimming or crawling out again, so easily. Leave the hazards of weak ice to the creatures adapted to meet them, to the creatures to which weak ice is no hazard at all.

•　　•　　•

I learned early in my teens that no camp could be enjoyable without a very minimum of conveniences, no matter how beauteous the scenery nor how otherwise satisfactory the purposes of the camp.

When I was fifteen, I stayed out of school the first half of December to trap on the marshes about the home farm, and I winter-camped alone in a tent. I have many memories of that camping, of cutting dead ash to burn in a folding sheet-iron stove, of my first profitable fur-trapping, of youthful inexperience, of loneliness, and, most of all, of what marshes could be in winter.

The weather showed characteristic Dakota variability for early December. A thaw took the snow off ice and ground, leaving mud on land, water over ice. Then, there was snow, and the lake ice boomed, and the cold awakened me in the night as I lay in my outdoor clothes under the blankets. I rebuilt the fire in the sheet-iron stove and shivered over it while listening to the coyotes. They seemed to be all around the tent, but, when I looked out through the flap, I could see that they could not be nearer than some hilltops, two hundred yards away. The sky was starry, and the sparkle of the stars over the new snow had an impersonality that left me feeling that it was up to me to take care of my own self.

I think it was then that I lost most of the nonsense I ever had in my head concerning moods of Nature, of winter weather, or any other kind of weather, ever being other than impersonal. The coyotes sounded ecstatic, but Nature was not being kind to them and cruel to me when my feet ached as I huddled as close to the stove as I could get without burning my clothes. The coyotes simply had more than I had at that time to cope with unfeeling phenomena. With recognition of the impersonality of natural forces, I could love the out-of-doors as it was, but with growing realism and awareness of the things to avoid if I wanted to stay comfortable and out of trouble.

I will confess that I got into numerous camping ordeals—if not actual danger—before I learned better. In time, my camping became so systematized that little was likely to go wrong. There might still be problems, as when the violence of a rain storm soaked everything even in a tent that by practical standards could be called water-proof. There might still be problems of keeping perishable food fresh or getting food or having a satisfactory water supply. It might be hard to keep from becoming too tired of camping itself at times of no feasible or desirable alternatives. Camping, by its nature, cannot be expected to compete with indoor living in terms of indoor comforts, but, done right, it should not be a hardship for healthy people—especially for healthy young people.

When I was young and camp life was daily routine for me for weeks or months at a stretch, I did not care about minor inconveniences and discomforts. Now, when I need to camp, I still do it, and, if I have something troublesome to put up with at a camp, I do that as well as I can, but any pride that I once felt in demonstrating ability to "take it" has long grown thin. In my middle age, I keep remembering how good the fresh eggs and meat-counter steaks of civilization can taste after prolonged sessions with pancakes and canned food—also the pleasantness of indoor rooms after outdoor activities. I am quite capable of plain weak-fleshed enjoyment of camp gadgets that make camping less like camping. I like to think of the sort of place where one might rest well and hang up wet garments to dry, a place designed for ease in cooking and keeping clean.

I wholly agree with the view of conservationists that there are places having wilderness values where roads and trailers would be out of place, quite out of key, and that such places should be kept road-less and trailer-less. I agree with my friend, the late Aldo Leopold, that camping *can* become overmuch an art of gadgetry and that a trailer *can* cap the pyramid of banalities in outdoor living in places where there are too many trailers. But, when a choice comes down to a personal basis for people who love the out-of-doors and who are no longer young, a trailer can have its talking points.

For my wife and me, for that nebulous future when we hope to be able to do things more leisurely and to do more that we want to do, maybe we can have a trailer somewhere during the flight seasons of the waterfowl. Maybe we can park our trailer beside a Dakota or a Canadian marsh, not in the remotest of wildernesses but away from the travel routes of large numbers of people. Our dream camps do not need to have complete solitude but they need some of the values of solitude, along with glacial marsh scenery and, yes, indeed, the minks and the muskrats . . . coyotes in the hills . . . and ducks . . . and ducks . . . and ducks . . .

9. *of marshes and peace of mind*

At times, one of man's greater needs is freedom from himself, and this freedom is likely to be increasingly threatened by population and economic pressures, by dogmas of organizations exalting power and bigness, and by old ideas that Nature exists only to be conquered. The trapper or the ex-trapper or the frank recluse is not alone in needing, on occasion, freedom from man to escape being psychologically overwhelmed by Man as a mass phenomenon.

Love of naturalness, of open skies and shady forests, of land and water and solitude and living things, is depicted over and over again in the world's literature and art, from long before the Christian era. It is known under many names or under no articulated names at all —by savages who can put little in words or who have in mind mystical deities of woods, waters, or mountains, and by persons of the most modern viewpoints who love the out-of-doors for what it is, all or part.

I do not forget that the outspokenly practical can dominate personal decisions in choices between natural values and material objectives, nor that appreciation of beauty can even be so restricted to the man-made as to leave with some people little or no concept of the beauties of anything else. Still, usually, there are some people in any community who at times prefer solitude or the company of a close friend amid surroundings that are too rocky or too wet to cultivate or otherwise "develop."

Wilderness and related outdoor values may not offset all of the worries and frustrations to which civilized man is subject, but they help. I would say that cherishing them can be among the experiences redeeming human life from futilities and conceits. The receptive person can thus better see himself, his life, and his problems within a framework of universal order, of permanent physical realities, of evolutionary trends, and of the great phenomena of Life.

In our north-central region, a glacial marsh is one type of predominantly native wilderness that we usually can retain after all of the others are lost in a thickly settled community—if we as the public really want to.

• • •

There is the question of what constitutes wholesome experience on or about a marsh, the question of what is acceptable conduct and its relation to human self-respect and peace of mind.

Let us further consider the duck hunting that provides so much motivation for people being on marshes during the fall months. In my younger years, when I did so much of it, hunting could be either enjoyable or otherwise, or both. At times, I had to work so hard to get the game needed for the table that it was no sport to hunt. At other times, when on trips in company with other hunters, I had to (or felt that I had to) continue shooting much longer than I wanted to, merely to bring in the legal bag limit thought essential to social standing.

I felt long ago that this old bag limit philosophy was pernicious, but it took me years thereafter to mature sufficiently to dare to show up in public without a bag limit after a hunt if I had any chance of getting the limit. I still do not like to come off a marsh during the hunting season and be looked over by hunters if I patently have been hunting and do not have in possession a creditable bag of ducks. Maybe this reflects a lingering immaturity, but I still know the feeling.

The low bag limits of recent years have, indeed, increased my enjoyment of duck hunting in a number of ways, chiefly in that they work for a desirable moderation, not only as concerns the ducks but also the duck hunters. A bag limit of four or five ducks in a day is large enough to give satisfaction at an ordinary family table as well as a tangible incentive for an autumnal outing on a marsh. Under modern Iowa conditions, it can still be difficult enough to obtain (except on those rather exceptional days when a hunter has repeated opportunities for shotgun range shooting) but still is small enough to be within possibility now and then. Some of my late-year duck hunts that I remember for their enjoyability were those during which I shot my four-bird bag limit fairly soon after going out, and, having made certain of my passport to respectable notice among my peers, then spent a couple of hours poking around amid pleasurable surroundings, possibly even being lazy. When I think of this, I do not have to go much further to think that the hunting itself need not be essential to peace of mind on a marsh, provided that things are otherwise right.

There is nothing like irritation to ruin the enjoyment of a marsh outing. The me-firsters, the bigots, and the litterers can find the marshes, too, and may claim rights to courtesies they are unwilling to return. When our civilization is accompanied by an improvement of public manners in the out-of-doors, perhaps we may have something like reciprocal courtesy and earn a little more of the peace of mind we seek.

Hunters may abuse each other over who shot a duck, and there may be arguments over hunting blinds, parking places, and personalities. Personal frictions may be, if anything, still more unpleasant when the economics of fur-trapping are involved, with still greater possibilities for actual violence and dirty work. Trouble-making, thievery, or vandalism are the same unattractive attributes of some people everywhere, on or off a marsh, but my feeling is that their incidence in marsh users is less than in the general public. Maybe I am ascribing redeeming influences to the marsh that it does not have in unromantic actuality. Still, I think that most hunters, trappers, and those who genuinely love marshes are fundamentally decent.

Personal rough edges and misunderstandings surely underlie some of the human frictions that can detract from the peace of mind of fundamentally decent people. There are people who just do not know that they are offending, and I do not mean the mere violators of the elaborate or whimsical codes that some sporting groups devise and try to foist on the rest of the world.

I had this impressed upon me rather recently while hunting on one of the state-owned public shooting grounds of northern Iowa. I was stalking some baldpates sitting out in shallow open water beyond a patchy fringe of bulrushes—working along, squatting down until my boot tops almost dipped water, keeping every bit of concealment between the ducks and me, waiting at intervals and moving as quietly as possible through mud and water. The next rush clump ahead was the place where I would stand up and flush the birds—and I was trembling with the fatigue of a long and slow and bent-over stalk. Then, I could see through openings between the rush stems that the ducks were swimming out of range, not directly away from me but away from another hunter who was casually walking in my direction. I knew that he saw me sneaking along, and I arose and left without saying anything but with impulses to say unkind things and many of them. I reminded myself that the day was beautiful and the marsh was beautiful.

I met the same man later at the parking place. He turned out to be a most agreeable person, who obviously knew nothing about hunting in any form. I realized then that he had spoiled my stalk inadvertently and I said nothing to him about it. He was out hunting, by himself, in his own way, enjoying the beautiful day and the beautiful marsh, and I felt genuinely glad that he was enjoying himself. On the way home, and at recurring times afterward, I felt gratified that, for once in my life, I had kept back angry words.

The practice of shooting at out-of-range ducks, or "sky-reaching," is sometimes prevalent about public marshes. It can be both so ruinous of sport and so shameful in terms of unnecessary wounding and waste as to be a main source of irritation to conscientious hunters. The lengths to which "sky-reachers" go in trying to scratch down birds may seem incredible to persons knowing anything about distances and shotgun patterns. Every flock or single duck coming within hundreds of yards may be shot at. I have often seen hunters one to two hundred yards or farther from me shoot at birds that were directly over *my* head, though out of *my* range, and endless stories may be heard about like displays of discourtesy.

If only inexperience is responsible for out-of-range shooting, much may be learned quickly by pacing off fifty yards (which is as far as anyone should be shooting at game with most shotguns), putting up an object the size of a duck's body, to see how large it looks at that distance, and then patterning the gun with game loads on it. Still more might be learned, also quickly, by patterning a game load at a hundred yards and noting how far apart the pellets strike, the varying sizes of gaps in the patterns, and, against a wooden backstop, how little the shot penetrate, compared with penetration at thirty-five or forty or fifty yards. Further thought about the size and location of vital areas of a duck's body in relation to shot patterns may round out the lesson.

I find no peace of mind when with men who make sweeping assertions that conservation agencies know nothing and never will and that this scientific stuff about wildlife management is baloney. Nor with the outdoorsmen who show their love for the natural out-of-doors and its creatures by demanding the extermination of hawks, crows, foxes, herons, minks, raccoons, snakes, the owls and eagles and pelicans, and everything else among wild flesh-eaters that some-one might nominate for a proscription list.

The pogroms that individuals or groups carry on against wild creatures may at times reflect something close to psychopathology. Barbarous and senseless punishments may be inflicted upon wild creatures for not conforming to the totally unnatural moral stand-ards that man sets up for them. We have the evangelists of the doc-trine that what is not game must be vermin. We have bloodletting crusades, with only the law (and not always that) restricting the scope of the killings. We have the he-man who can be so tender toward a plant-eater and so easily aroused to hatred of a flesh-eater merely because the latter lives in the only way it can be expected to live.

When outdoor places that have distinctive values chiefly for the reason that they may still have naturalness are made the scenes of such excesses, it is time for a little thought to be centered upon adaptations of living creatures for living and upon what ecologists call biotic communities. At least, a little thought might help, and it would not be inappropriate to think about what has value for whom.

It is not that all human interference with natural relationships intended in behalf of human interests must of itself be wrong. The wrongness lies in emotional extremes that can be especially unjusti-fiable when manifested by "throwing weight around" and spoiling the peace of other people in those parts of the out-of-doors that should be left for seekers after peace. Hunter, trapper, boater, pic-nicker, hiker, botanist, and birder, all have their own rights and also their own obligations toward other people. There is still guidance in the Golden Rule.

The litterer may be in a special class only in that he litters. A well-dressed couple may drive up to a bridge in a polished car and heave boxes of garbage into a gully or creek. Someone else may dispose of the material evidences of a drinking party by taking the bottles or cans out to the nearest country road. A family has a Sunday picnic and leaves everything there that it does not wish to take home—the familiar newspapers, paper plates, pickle jars, melon rinds, milk containers, cleansing tissues, and cigarette packages.

Littering is often regarded as a failing of only city people, but let no one deceive himself concerning this. Farmers, too, can be chronic litterers, and some of the junkiest places are those where city people practically never go—the camp grounds of real cowboys or the portage trails of real northerners. I have seen camp sites of hunters and trappers—of whom it could be said that they were genuine marsh men—that were left as messes by any definition.

The litterers that I have seen have not been, on the whole, persons of objectionable habits except for their littering. I think that such negligence in outdoor manners may be something that has grown on us over recent decades, to the extent that it is now being referred to as a national disgrace. The littering of today is partly due to more people having more to litter with. When I was young, there was not so very much that picnickers using household cloth and tableware would have along to leave behind them except food remnants, possibly bottles, possibly a few cans or paper sacks or some wrapping paper. Some of the present-day problem may represent a cumulative phenomenon, some littering resulting from places already being so littered up over the years that even conscientious people feel that a little more added could not make any difference.

I ascribe my own early attitude on littering to the influence of editorials and articles read in outdoor magazines when a youngster. I must say that my camps had ways of being more or less littered while I lived in them, but I liked to look at a camp site when leaving it and to see nothing there but the wet ashes of a little fire and a little area of trampled ground and vegetation, with maybe some heads and entrails of game left off to the side as an offering for wild creatures. The convenient slogans to the effect that a place should be left as clean as found did help to keep my early attitude virtuous in this respect whenever my temptation was to be careless. After the good habits became set for life, I simply thought of leaving places as I wanted them to be left.

The one thing that is *not* hopeless about the littered vistas of the American outdoors is a growing and articulate public resentment. One nationally influential group after another is putting on anti-littering campaigns. These campaigns seem to be vigorous and sustained, and they surely should contribute to outdoor betterment as long as they are directed primarily against littering. I am not backing any clean-up craze that merely accelerates destruction of native

vegetation, fallen logs, or other naturalness in places where naturalness belongs; but I believe, if the public can work together toward
sound anti-littering objectives, that we can do something worth
doing. It is the business of all of us as citizens, or it should be, and it
is time for improvement to be coming along.

•   •   •   •   •

One thinks of the end of a day as being a time for peace of mind,
and a sunset may have not only its own beauty but its symbolism of
peace.

My memories of sunsets are not confined to marshes, but it has
been on marshes that I have been aware of some of the feelings
coming nearest to complete peace of mind of which I seem capable.
Others have had similar experiences. I think of an internationally

of marshes and peace of mind   *121*

known sportsman, an industrialist, who, for years, planned vacations so that he could spend part of them on an Iowa marsh during the trapping season. When asked if he were not becoming too old for that sort of thing, if he might not die sometime out there on the marsh, he asked in his turn: "What better place is there to die?"

Air and water do not need to be quiet to induce peace of mind if one be receptive, but there is symbolism in Nature's quiet, too. The reference to still waters in the Twenty-third Psalm, the final paragraphs of Longfellow's *Hiawatha,* and countless other passages in our literature reveal fundamental longings of people everywhere.

My own memories of sunsets and peace of mind in wetland settings differ greatly in details. They include memories of hunters poling in to shore, of kidding and laughter; of trappers almost flying over the ice in boats on runners, coming in to rest, warm up, eat, and talk; of scenes with no other people or traces of other people in sight.

I think of one in which I was a predator. Late one afternoon, by the most careful crawling through marshy cover and over wide, bare stretches of mud, I worked right into the midst of a small flock of feeding mallards. I had to walk around the marsh to reach the canoe and then return over the water to pick up the birds that the shooting gave me. Before undertaking the hour and a half stalk, I had thought that I probably could not get away with it, and then, in the mellowness of accomplishment, I shook the water off the mallards and laid them on their backs in the bottom of the canoe, and looked upon them and across the marsh toward the sunset. A couple of small islands were reflected on the water, and the sunset colored the whole western view.

I was anything but a predator while watching another sunset, when ducks were alighting by the hundreds in one of the few marshes having water during a great drought. Those ducks were little more than population remnants, and, at that time, I was doing all that I could to discourage anyone from duck hunting. I stayed at the marsh edge until I could no longer see anything of the ducks and could hear only their calls and the sounds of wings in air and splashing in water.

I have memories of other sunsets at times when I was simply living my life, such as it then happened to be. I might be driving home the cattle along the lake shore back on the South Dakota farm. Or, as a biologist, I might be making a marsh-edge camp before dark and trying also to keep track of the fighting and wandering of muskrats out on the ice at the time of a population crisis. I might be trying to catch fish for food and not doing well at it. I might be sitting in a car writing up field notes or just sitting and watching.

I often recall the coming of a night on Upper Red Lake in northern Minnesota, long ago when I was young. I was returning to my trapping headquarters on the Tamarack River after having gone to the largest town within reach by canoe to buy a half-case of shotgun shells and several crates of dried prunes.

By late afternoon, the water was becoming quiet and, toward sunset, it was smooth—mile after mile of it—with a slow and rhythmic undulation. I still had a couple of hours of paddling ahead of me to reach the cabin, and ice crystals were forming on the burnished water, tiny needles growing as the sun went down. I kept dipping the paddle as fast as I could and still get full power out of it. Dip, pull, scull, over and over, my knees spread and braced in the center of the canoe, the sound of my heart and breathing mingling with the sound of swirling water about the paddle.

As dusk came, the ice needles tinkled with the rise and fall of water over the lodged driftwood out from the beach and hissed as the canoe rode through them. I was happy, though a little uncertain. I knew that the hissing would grow louder and that, by the time I reached the Tamarack, there might be thin ice to break —perhaps just a little ice, enough to outline the wake of the canoe and to wear away some paint without actually wearing through the canvas. Perhaps the ice would be cutting-ice before I could find a place having a land trail to the cabin. When I reached a trail, I could leave the canoe and pack home in the darkness the precious crates of prunes.

That memory is one of peace and of problems. The problems were not overwhelming, but there were the uncertainty and the awareness of things still to be done. So it seems to be with man almost always, almost anywhere. Peace of mind exists, or can exist, but I do not know how much any of us can attain any complete peace. It seems such a relative quality, whether that be due to me, to the nature of the human mind, or to the nature of peace, itself. Anyway, I can find some peace in thoughts of water seeking its own levels, of buds unfolding, of fruits ripening, and of wild things staying wild; and I think that the outdoor values that have meant so much to my life are among those worth preserving in modern civilization and those that every well-intentioned person should have a right to share if he wishes.

10. *of marshes and man and harmonious use*

The great cartoons of my fellow-Iowan, J. N. ("Ding") Darling, were prodding the public conscience on land abuses—pollution, erosive farming, excessive deforestation and drainage—long before I became a resident of the state. They depicted the incongruities of wasting what we have at home and then expecting to go somewhere else for the enjoyment of hunting, fishing, and outdoor beauty. Many of them dealt with drainage versus marshes and marsh life.

When I ponder my wetland philosophy, I recognize that some drainage to eliminate troublesome wet spots can be well conceived —always providing that it does not go too far. But drainage does have ways of going too far! We have long gotten past the stage of being able to afford more drainage excesses. Concerning the North American marsh situation, Harold Titus published an informative article entitled, "Tomorrow is too late!" The glacial marshes of Iowa may now be considered drained, except for the marshes that are state-owned and a few undrained marshes still in private ownership. As far north as The Pas, in Manitoba, agricultural drainage has eliminated, or is threatening, some of the best waterfowl and fur areas of the continent.

It is time for a reversal in the drainage trend. As members of a presumably rational and enlightened society, do we need to let the destruction of our wetland values continue as long as someone feels able personally to profit thereby?

•   •   •

In some regions, the recommended types of agricultural land use may favor (or at least permit) retention of marshes. In 1953, I heard an illustrated lecture by J. W. Kimball, then of the Office of River Basin Studies, U. S. Fish and Wildlife Service, about the superb waterfowl breeding grounds known as the pothole country of Minnesota and the Dakotas. A large proportion of this pothole country is rolling terrain, with the fertile soils on the hills being shallow and erodable, and for which agriculturists advocate grass-land farming. At present, the temptation for farmers of the pothole country to cultivate the hills is pronounced and will remain so as long as the regional economy is on a grain-raising basis. Kimball cited, in his lecture, researches showing big differences in value of beef produced on poor and on fertile soils and concluded that a shift to grassland farming should be encouraged in the pothole country before loss of the soil fertility of the hills resulted from cultivation. Benefits to marshes and marsh wildlife to be gained through such a system of grassland farming would still depend upon exactly what was done or not done. A landholder might still, as through over-grazing, wreck both soil and marsh values without having any land under cultivation, but the over-all application of sound methods of husbandry *could* be compatible with preservation of marsh values.

*The role of marshes and lakes in maintaining ground water levels of a region does not seem fully understood. Perhaps few acceptable generalizations go much further than "It depends . . ." Nevertheless, the matter of sinking water tables is becoming so vital to our civilization that we as a public may properly review our programs for draining surface waters to see whether they might have their reckless aspects from this standpoint, alone. I have lived long enough to observe public reactions to dust bowls and dry wells and to wet years, alike. Nothing so much as a water shortage resurrects the slogan, "Keep the water on the land," but, when we again have water on the land, how quickly it becomes something to get rid of! Here, again, it should not seem inappropriate for the American public to strive for balanced judgment rather than to

swing back and forth from extreme to extreme in our handling of water, even though we may not know all the answers and may never know them.

Drainage systems that channel surface waters into streams having tendencies to flood, and to contribute to flood damage farther downstream, may not be considered sound, irrespective of how advantageous they may be for certain property owners along the way. Drainage into reservoirs can be better engineering, especially if the watershed be suitably protected from erosion. I can conceive of projects of this sort that could well safeguard the economic interests of a community. But I still do not intend to endorse the drainage of our remaining marshes merely because drainage could be accomplished with economic and engineering propriety.

The last time that I visited a once-familiar area in eastern South Dakota, I saw that the scattered little marshes had been drained, that their contrasts of green rushes and open water had changed to

of marshes and man and harmonious use   127

cultivated fields and pastures—more fields and pastures added to panoramas of fields and pastures. The drainage was, I know, a splendid demonstration of technology. Farm income had been increased on the drained lands. No problems of erosion or flood control had been aggravated by the drainage. The networks of tile converged at a lake, which was larger and deeper than before. The water was still in the country. The drained land included some that was not actually marshland. Places were drained where a tractor could bog down in ordinary farm work, or where the water would be held long enough after a rain to drown the corn, or where the land was too wet to grow anything that anyone—even a naturalist—wanted and still not wet enough to be any good as a marsh.

Yet, so far as my ideas of marsh values were concerned, the over-all impacts of that drainage program were saddening. The little potholes and sloughs and outlying marshes have an importance to the waterfowl breeding grounds of the north-central region that is far out of proportion to their acreages and to the volumes of water impounded in them. They may be especially important as breeding grounds when occurring as clusters of wet areas. Their loss to waterfowl is not made up by concentrating their water in another place. The concentration of the drained-off water in the above instance did, in fact, detract from the value that the receiving body originally had for marsh-dwelling wildlife. At the time of my last visit, it had lost much of its emergent vegetation from flooding. It had a dilute population of terns, blackbirds, shore birds, and bank-dwelling muskrats, a closely grazed pasture ashore. There were the melodious upland plovers whistling from fence posts and numbers of ducks sitting around—about as many ducks as I would have expected to see at that place, anyway, if the surrounding potholes had been intact and populated by their own ducks. The receiving body of water had pondweeds and other duck foods and other values as waterfowl environment—surely more than if it also had been drained—but, as waterfowl environment, it was no substitute for the sacrificed potholes.

It should be proper here to discuss ways of making money from marshes other than by draining them. In this connection, the econ-omy-minded should consider the possibility that even modest returns from natural marshes might still be "good business," even strictly from a money-making standpoint. At least, a natural marsh does not call for large expenditures for drainage if it is not to be drained. (Many of the South Dakota pothole owners admit that they would

of marshes and man and harmonious use

not participate in the draining if they did not virtually have it paid for by agricultural agencies.)

Apart from limited commercial or utility harvesting of plant products from marshes (reeds for thatching, peat, marsh hay, wild rice as a delicacy, aquatic nursery items to sell for transplanting, etc.), the money-making potentialities of marsh management are somewhat restricted to game and fur resources.

Leasing of hunting or trapping rights can be big business in some localities—so much so that the main livelihood of some communities may be derived therefrom, with marshes being regarded in the sense of special croplands and zealously safeguarded from damage or deterioration. Managed marshes may be labeled "fur farms," "hunting clubs," "wildlife management areas," or in other ways. They may be managed privately or by state, provincial, federal, or other public agencies. In size, they range up to hundreds of thousands of acres. They may be subject to management that can be everything from merely keeping them wet to modern techniques of the greatest diversity.

Management of marshes as marshes has grown into a science of its own, the literature of which would astound people accustomed to thinking only of conventional land uses. It has its unknowns and complexities, and disappointments in marsh management can occur the same as can disappointments in other types of land use; but readers wishing to investigate can easily learn that marsh management for game or fur is no longer in its groping stages. By now, the marsh manager knows something about the needs of the muskrats and ducks and of the upland wildlife coming to the marsh edges, of the living requirements of bulrush and cattail and arrowhead and pondweed, of marsh soils and the microscopic life of marshes, and of the marsh as a biological entity.

• • • •

Conscientious people may have their objections to hunting or trapping as forms of marsh use. As one who has done much hunting and trapping, I may be suspected of having my own biases in favor of hunting and trapping, and I do have them.

To some people, whose love of outdoor values is unquestionably strong, it seems incomprehensible that anyone loving wild creatures could kill them. I think that I understand their viewpoint, at least in part, although I do not share it more than in part. Some killing

of marshes and man and harmonious use

may be entirely compatible with great love for the wildlife that may thus be killed, or, at any rate, with great love of the Nature to which the wildlife belongs. There have been, and are, hunters and trappers among our most sincere and selfless conservationists.

Hunting and trapping were among my major activities in my earlier years because that was what I liked to do and had opportunities to do and because I was thereby afforded an acceptable excuse for spending time in the out-of-doors. As long as my hunting and trapping yielded edible game and salable fur, I had a reply for the practical-minded. My being in this socially and economically defensible position was important to me, as one reared at a time and place where dollars were rather scarce and where the old standby virtues of thrift and industry were respected.

For me, as one who killed for a livelihood for years, the act of killing was commonly merely incidental to the harvesting of food or fur. I regarded myself as a predator living off the land and killed, when killing was to be done, with about the same feelings as I picked berries, as neatly and efficiently as I could. Most of my killing that was not done in connection with *bona fide* wildlife harvesting was shooting jackrabbits and ground-squirrels during the summer months of my South Dakota years, and this was done for sport as well as for rifle and pistol practice.

The years have brought some modifications in my personal attitude toward killing wild animals. If there be what I consider reason for it, I can still kill ducks for a duck dinner or the moles or pocket gophers that may be doing damage in the garden or set traps for the harvesting of hundreds of muskrats from a marsh—and do it matter-of-factly or even enjoyably. However, I no longer care to use living animals just as targets, and my inclinations are to leave the so-called varmints in peace unless circumstances demand otherwise.

I am not aware of any feeling of guilt when thinking about shooting bag limits of twenty-five ducks in my younger years as a hunter and trapper. I do not feel that there was anything *then* reprehensible about trying to shoot selectively for the choicer ducks, nor about living upon ducks, when that was possible, for months out of each year. That was before the ducks lost so much of their breeding grounds, before the public took up duck hunting on such a big scale, and before the hunting so thoroughly sprinkled strategic marsh and lake bottoms with lead shot to be later ground away in duck gizzards.

But, what the waterfowl could easily endure then in the way of legal gun fire does not change the modern need for tightened hunting regulations. Nor does it change the fact that even a four-bird bag limit or a short open season can be too much for species that should not be shot at all.

How many ducks do we now have coming down in the fall through a gantlet of a couple of million American duck hunters? Considerably fewer than a hundred million at worst and not so very many more than a hundred million at best, according to the figures of the U. S. Fish and Wildlife Service. With a daily bag limit of four, it would not take the successful shooting of an indefinite number of bag limits on the part of the majority of a couple of million hunters practically to eliminate game ducks from North America in a single shooting season, especially if we consider the losses incidental to public hunting that sometimes exceed the number brought to bag!

There are some realities here that should not be ignored. Whether due to excessive hunting pressures or not, the duck populations of some of the South Dakota marshlands familiar to me since my youth have declined during recent decades even faster than their environments have declined. In the late forties, I saw breeding populations of perhaps two to five pairs on South Dakota marshes where up to a dozen pairs could have been expected thirty years before. This was the impression gained from county-to-county traveling in what had been among the best breeding grounds of the Dakotas.

Only on wildlife refuges did breeding duck populations of the late forties remind me of what had been commonplace on the Dakota marshes of the early and mid-twenties. From what we now know of the role of tradition in bringing ducks back to breed in the areas in which they were reared, it would seem that more birds returned to nest on the refuges because the refuges provided a better chance for the birds reared there to survive the hunting season. Very competent investigations on the prairie breeding grounds suggest that hunting can be especially deadly when borne by bewildered young ducks still frequenting the marshes where they were reared. If these young ducks receive protection until they leave on their fall migration, their chances for survival appear to be appreciably improved, despite their being subject to hunting after leaving. Effective refuge areas may therefore be expected to retain higher breeding populations of ducks better than comparable marshlands on which large proportions of the locally reared young birds may be killed soon after the opening of the hunting season.

The consequences of modern gun fire to a game species may be negligible or they may be overwhelming, depending upon how resilient and well-established the species may be and upon what else may be happening. Continued shooting of precariously situated waterfowl may be one of the big problems in the wise and reasonable use of marshes and marsh resources. A hunting public unskilled in identifying ducks in flight may not enthusiastically receive special regulations applying to certain species; but, if special regulations do lessen the kill of redheads, canvasbacks, and other threatened forms, that is something gained, even though some specially protected birds may still be shot by mistake or by intentional violation.

(No one need remind me that hunters are not invariably well-intentioned. In years when redheads were legally protected, some hunters deliberately shot ducks as they came along and avoided legal responsibilities by discarding their redhead victims. Years later, some hunters responded to a four-duck bag limit by knocking down several times that number, taking their pick of the four finest and leaving the others to rot on the marsh!)

Complexities in regulations for hunting waterfowl may perhaps be inevitable in view of the complexities of waterfowl problems over the continent. Situations may vary with species, years and seasons of years, localities, flyways, centers of human population, hunting and land-use practices, and conflicting policies in public agencies. We may have a management picture complicated by commercial interests of many kinds (including the illegitimate), waterfowl depredations upon crops in concentration areas, weather, and the well-known drainage of wetlands—and a hunting public that can sometimes be more than a little inclined to invent panaceas and comfortable slogans, to do what it wants to do, and to overestimate the share of the out-of-doors to which the purchase of a hunting license entitles it to have.

As a duck hunter, I can still say that hunting regulations should favor the species of ducks that need favoring rather than the hunters, that the burden of proof in liberalizing hunting regulations in favor of the hunters should fall upon the liberalizers, and that such proof should be based upon tangible evidence. If increased hunting restrictions make sense, we should by all means have them—up to and including totally closed seasons on endangered species of waterfowl or even (if necessary) upon all waterfowl as long as any need for such drastic action remains apparent. A totally closed season, in the modern science of game or wildlife management, is a tool to be used with discrimination rather than as an end in itself. It should have its place in the management of waterfowl as well as in the management of pheasants, deer, muskrats, beavers, and the rest of the game species for which closed seasons may be prescribed.

Like waterfowl hunting, fur-trapping has, I would say, a rightful place in the management and utilization of North American marshes. Like hunting, trapping can be one of the main reasons why some important marshes may and should escape drainage.

Management of migratory waterfowl and fur-bearers may be mutually compatible in most respects, on the same marsh and as different yet complementary parts of the same management program. We need not here go into the technology of waterfowl or fur management on Northern Hemisphere wetlands. Let it only be reiterated that there can be such a thing as multiple use of a marsh as well as of arable dry land.

Headwork is called for in multiple uses of wetlands, too, including headwork in the harvesting of fur-bearers. The sins of excessive trapping pressures can come home to roost on a quite personal basis. So can mistakes in attempting to "stockpile" live muskrats on a marsh, to the extent that underharvesting invites epidemics and overexploitation of marsh vegetation by the muskrats.

Like hunting, trapping can have its abuses. Cruelties in taking fur-bearers in steel traps give rise to many of the objections people feel toward trapping as a legitimate form of marsh use. At their worst, the cruelties of steel traps can be sickening to contemplate, and no defense whatever need be offered for some of the things that some trappers do. But marsh trapping, employing well-tested methods and equipment and featuring merciful drown sets under conditions favoring their use, need not have much cruelty in it. Even when the water may be too shallow to drown with regularity animals caught in ordinary steel traps, the use of modern "stop-loss" designs of steel traps (now standard products of the major trap companies) promotes drowning of at least muskrats and minks in surprisingly little water—at times, in only a few inches over the bottom mud.

As with hunters who lose crippled game now and then despite skill and care, the best of trappers can have an occasional trapped muskrat or other victim mangle itself in its struggles, even in sets

of marshes and man and harmonious use

intended to drown. Such accidents cannot be wholly prevented by any methods of which I know, and I do not think that they should be played up in arguments against trapping as long as their occurrence is kept down as much as possible. In recent muskrat trapping experiments on an Iowa marsh having very shallow water, the incidence of animals mangled in the jaws of steel traps of "stop-loss" designs was only about three percent; and, under trapping conditions more conducive to drowning, the performances of the "stop-losses" were humane according to any workable criteria for fur-harvesting.

Also, as with hunters, the skill and attitudes of the trappers make most of the difference between the degrees of respectability to be seen in wildlife harvests on north-central marshes. The wrong kind of hunter shoots into flocks at long range with large shot in the hope of bringing down a bird by a chance hit or just shoots and shoots at whatever flies, within range or out of range, even though birds fall in thick vegetation from which they cannot be retrieved, and even though two or even more birds are lost for each one bagged. Among trappers, we have those who set traps in almost any place, with little regard for whatever creatures may get into them, whether victims suffer needlessly or not, whether traps may be visited tomorrow, next week, some day, or not at all.

While well-considered, enforceable regulations certainly may have value in correcting both hunting and trapping abuses, the best remedies seem to lie in enlightened public opinion. More and more of the conservation work done by public agencies is educational, and it seems gradually to be improving hunting and trapping practices. There is nothing like the esteem of one's fellows to put virtue into places where it is not cherished as a sufficient reward in itself!

Unfortunately, youngsters, for reasons of immaturity and inexperience, may have some of the worst faults as hunters or trappers, but, insofar as these same youngsters are among the people for whom a wholesome interest in hunting or trapping (together with other outdoor pursuits) can be of the greatest importance, it is up to us to be patient with them. Youngsters can learn the right things fast under guidance.

For that matter, it is of the youngsters that I think when feeling depressed because of the continuing shrinkage of wildlife environment as more and more land is put into agricultural production—as marsh bottoms turn into more corn- or wheatfields, as almost every odd corner having any wildness is plowed, cleared, or pastured, or slicked up and deprived of any wildness that it ever had. For many youngsters, hunting, trapping, fishing, or kindred outdoor interests may mean nothing that they would ever miss; but, for others, deprivation of opportunities for enjoyment of such things may be a great loss and a loss that they do not deserve.

•   •   •   •

In my opinion, while exploitative forms of marsh use such as hunting and trapping are justifiable as long as they are decently done and limited to reasonable use of renewable natural resources, they should not be overemphasized. Non-exploitative enjoyments of the marsh, itself, are those deserving of being called "the higher use." They are among those best adapted to year-round use and even to mass-use, if it comes to that, in settled communities. The non-exploitative are the only ones permissible or within reason on or about many of the marshes still to be found in metropolitan areas, the marshes of wildlife refuges, the privately owned marshes on which owners do not want exploitative pursuits.

Much of my purpose in writing this book is to encourage wider participation by the public in the quieter uses of marshes, the walking along shore or the slipping of a canoe around rush clumps, with due care not to disturb wild creatures to their disadvantage.

Speed-boating is hardly an appropriate use for a beautiful natural marsh, for it is disruptive of the tranquility that should characterize a marsh during at least the breeding season of marsh wildlife. Then, too, it has a way of leading to agitation for clearing of large marshy areas of so-called weeds (meaning any natural vegetation, emergent or submerged, that can get in the way) to facilitate more and faster speed-boating. I would not detract from the pleasure of those who enjoy speed-boating, but wish that they would do it on open water lakes lined with summer cottages and concessions and otherwise developed for resort trade rather than to attempt to make race courses out of marshes.

I like good firearms and the right kind of shooting, and my wish is not to discourage similar interests on the part of the public; but I never feel easy about the combination of guns and public about a marsh except during the hunting season for game—and not always then! Too much of the time, the public simply cannot be trusted when firearms are taken along on a Sunday outing or

of marshes and man and harmonious use   135

an afternoon or evening picnic. My meaning will surely be clear to people who have had gun muzzles waved in their faces, listened to glancing bullets, walked amid bullet-broken glass, or conjectured as to what wild or domestic creatures were serving as the shooters' targets. (It is not that my own past has been of complete faultlessness in this respect, for, as an immature, I sometimes did things with firearms—as well as with money, axes, canoes, automobiles, horses, fists, and a too-ready tongue—of which, as an adult, I am not the least proud.) I would rather see the public carrying binoculars or cameras.

My mind keeps returning to walks along lake shores or among the marshes and hills of the old home neighborhood in South Dakota, with a rifle or pistol being almost a part of me. A little shooting at a blaze on a tree trunk or at a row of small clam shells against a dirt backstop was almost a ritual. Still . . . I know what people *can* do with guns. One of the few ospreys that I ever saw about a familiar Iowa marsh was a shot bird lying on the shore.

If one must make a choice that can always be defended, target shooting probably belongs on a target range. This should not represent any intolerable restriction of personal liberties. My two favorite rifles, through which many thousands of carefully hand-loaded bullets have been fired, have almost never been fired away from a target range. They never killed anything, never endangered anything or anybody.

• • •

Some of the nostalgia that I feel for marshes that I have known traces back to childhood impressions of the once-unplowed moraines, of large tracts—several square miles in a block—of land not deemed fit for any agricultural use except haying or grazing. To impressions of hills with prairie chickens, of waters and skies with ducks, of badger holes and flint arrowheads and the deliciously chilling knowledge—to a child—of wolves being out there somewhere. To the wonder-years of waterfowl when, long before my own shoulder could take the recoil of a twelve-gauge black powder load, I watched the fire-flashes and white smoke of those loads as the menfolks hunted on the home farm marshes. In northern wildernesses, I feel nostalgia at the sight of a crumbling trapper's cabin. I know a couple of these on what are now heavily traveled routes for canoeists and sport fishermen, and they were not put there to attract tourists —though they may be left for that purpose. They are genuine remains of utility cabins, possibly datable to about the first of the century.

We hear the chant of the juggernautists that nothing can withstand man, that population pressures must force man eventually to use everything usable on earth for his support. We need not feel over-critical of man for looking out for his own interests, including means of livelihood, but neither need we commend his heavy-handedness in dealing with the exploited earth and with the other living things that belong on the earth, too. A philosophy of destruction of whatever happens to fall outside of their personal interests is no more admirable in present-day people than it was in their predecessors. When either individuals or groups lightly destroy what is precious to others, their arrogance in so doing can be even less admirable if they claim to be civilized and broad-minded.

Aldo Leopold observed the nostalgia, the passionate feeling of Germans for wildness, in a land populated to such a degree that making a daily living was a far more acute general problem than we have in North America. There are numerous places in the world where crowded and impoverished peoples, with toil and frugality essential to their living at all, do make sacrifices to preserve what they want. Some of these efforts have few counterparts in our more "practical" American communities, and we, as a public, could learn something from them about values going beyond physical necessities or comforts. I doubt that I would find my personal ideals of wildernesses fulfilled in many of these man-crowded lands, but there is inspiration in the example set by the people of a war-wrecked European city in refusing to cut a beloved forest for firewood despite their misery from cold. In the concluding paragraph of a famous textbook, Leopold also expressed himself to the effect that a truer test of American civilization would be the capacity of citizens to live at a high population density without befouling and denuding their environment rather than the mere attainment of a high density.

It is true, we may expect problems in our efforts to retain natural values. The same ducks and geese that, as species, may urgently need more protection from man than they may receive can still commit expensive crop depredations locally, as in grain fields that invite concentrations. So may sandhill cranes, and I have heard farmers agitating for a bounty on these wonderful birds in some of the few

places still having considerable numbers. I know what losses are from my own experience. One year on the South Dakota farm, severe winter weather caught my partner and me with about a third of our corn unpicked, and we decided to postpone the rest of the picking until spring. The mallards and geese settled in that field in the spring, and, when we were ready to resume picking, we found that we had no corn left to pick. That hurt where we could not afford to be hurt, but it would have hurt me infinitely more to have had spring without the mallards and the geese.

We may have problems with real complexities in mosquito control, but entomologists may obtain remarkably satisfactory results (I am not saying that it is always done or always can be done) with slight detriment to wetland values. We may have problems in weed control, but expert information is available as to how selective spraying can attain desirable objectives without undue sacrifices

of marshes and man and harmonious use

in other respects, without indiscriminate application of chemical weed-killers destroying harmless or valuable natural growths, marsh vegetation included. There can be more to meeting these problems than the unimaginative formulas of drain, drain or kill, kill.

A combination of skill, understanding, and desire to do the right thing is the best insurance against excesses in the management of wetlands as well as of anything else. It is the civilized answer to juggernaut philosophy, and an answer is needed.

We have the engineering and economic triumphs of intensified agriculture over the glaciated prairies and the push of human populations into areas that were remote from settlements a few decades ago, but the American public is, I think, awakening, becoming aroused about what we are wasting in making our undeniably substantial technological gains. The public can show interest in keeping marshes marshy.

The National Wildlife Federation, which chose "Save America's Wetlands" for the theme of its National Wildlife Week for 1955, has an affiliated membership of about three million. Minnesota and South Dakota—two states where drainage has been most rapid and threatening to remaining marshes in late years—are scenes of concerted action programs for the preservation of marshes. These programs work both to acquire marshes for public ownership and to encourage private landowners to manage what they have for wetland wildlife. Furthermore, as action programs, they have as participants not only state and federal conservation agencies, the Izaak Walton League, the American Legion, labor unions, newspapers, and like organizations, but also large-membership organizations dedicated to the specific objective of protecting and restoring marshes.

Glacial marshes are not the whole picture in modern life but they are part of it. I do not think that our public is going to be satisfied with a man-ordered world of cultivated fields and pastures and landscaping and roads and buildings; nor with a world so artificialized nearly everywhere that few people would stand much of a chance of finding anything different if they looked for it. As a people, we are not yet conditioned to regard spontaneous wildness as valueless in an advanced society, nor do I think we are going to be.

epilogue: of marshes and the laws of life

We may now consider a view that is held by many thoughtful people. It is not exclusively a view of professional ecologists and teachers, though ecologists and teachers are among those I have heard expressing it most frequently. A single sentence that paraphrases it might be that civilized man could show some civilization by preserving in as natural condition as possible representative types of the different plant and animal communities before they are lost.

Such would mean going farther than preserving the mountain tops that no one would find exploitable, the lands too rocky or otherwise unsuitable for cultivation, the forested lands too inaccessible for lumbering, and the odd pieces of land having slight economic value that "practical" man might not want. It would mean preservation of some places with the best timber or soils or building sites, some that could easily be plowed and kept plowed, some marshes that could be turned into cornfields. It would entail recognition of values other than the monetary.

Apart from any esthetic appreciation that ecologists may feel toward undespoiled wilderness preserves, including marshes, one of their chief motivations in preservation of wilderness is to safeguard areas where ancient interrelationships of plants, animals, soils, and climates may be studied. It is to safeguard areas where comparisons may be made between plants and animals subject to all degrees of human land use and those that live undisturbed (or relatively undisturbed) by man and man's. Their thesis is that important things may be learned about laws of life from wild populations living on wild areas.

At least some of us feel that an understanding of these laws is essential to human welfare, if for no other reason than to help man avoid the more basic of mistakes toward which he always seems to be heading. Enlightened peoples should ultimately learn what may be expected when human affairs and resources are mismanaged and learn something about the general landmarks to overwhelming situations without going all of the way.

The laws of life can, most assuredly, catch up with man. We need not restrict our comparisons to the cataclysmic, though it may be a temptation to compare a botulism outbreak among massed water birds or an epidemic in a dense muskrat population with human plagues in the cities of medieval Europe, or to compare other sweeping tragedies among wild populations with the impacts upon human populations of Asiatic famines, volcanic action, earthquakes, or even the new-style cataclysm introduced at Hiroshima. The less spectacular day-by-day parallels would seem to be the most informative concerning the fundamental principles that Life lives by.

In my own professional studies of animal populations, I have never felt more aware of parallels between human and nonhuman responses to natural crises than when working on marshes. No species has taught me more about parallels that I think man should be familiar with than has the muskrat, a living entity that, like man, has problems of living with what endowments it possesses, of meeting vicissitudes, and of getting along with its fellows.

•   •   •

Let us say that we have a marsh and that on it live many muskrats. The muskrats of our marsh are not so numerous that they occupy every square yard or consume the entire food supply. Seldom do we find that sort of thing in mammal populations even at times of acute crowding. Let us say that the muskrats of our marsh are not anywhere nearly as numerous in terms of animals per acre as muskrats could be on marshes and that, on our marsh, they are not as numerous as on some other marshes in their neighborhood.

Nevertheless, matters are not as they once were on our marsh. Human society in like circumstances could find cause to deplore the prevalence of unrest and crime, the lack of opportunity for youth, and the race suicide implied by the falling birth rate.

Patriarchal muskrats do not talk of the prosperous days when their fellows had better dispositions and when families of fifteen or twenty go-getting youngsters were raised in a season instead of a trifling half-dozen that are afraid of their own shadows. They do not ask what the marsh is coming to, within a life-span of its development from the jungle of cattails and bulrushes the settlers went forth to conquer. They do not advocate economic systems operating on the principle of eternal acceleration. Nor do they warn that, unless the community regains the initiative and virtues of its founders, the marsh might as well be left to the minks.

Nor do they invest their racial enemies, the minks, with demoniacal attributes and blame them for all of the trouble of muskratdom. They do not like minks, and no one should expect them to, muskrats being muskrats and minks being minks; but the muskrats at least cannot fairly be charged with the greater follies of scapegoat philosophies.

Insofar as the muskrats are what man calls lower animals, they simply live as their forebears lived, with what they have, for themselves.

The population does not share alike either its resources or its troubles. Some families live in relative security, their young and the young of their neighbors growing up together in the cattails that stretch out beyond the lodges. Some families live in rush and reed clumps of the open-water center, and these families are favorably situated except during storms. Elsewhere, some families get along passably well, and others do not.

Covering the shallows at one side of the marsh, the richest stand of food plants for miles attracts muskrats that wedge in their breeding territories wherever space can be had. It is a busy but not a happy place, and most muskrats do little moving far from what they claim and can hold for themselves.

About the edges of the crowded territories, what a muskrat does is conditioned by what its neighbors permit. Even when acquaintances permit close approach, or when there is some common sharing of marshy tracts or habitations, stranger sooner or later meets stranger if a muskrat ventures on past its neighbors' territories.

When the cattails of the crowded shallows begin to give out, whether because of overuse or for reasons for which the muskrats are not responsible, the residents do not actually starve. They merely

grow more irritable and inflict more drastic penalties for trespassing and do more trespassing, themselves.

Strangers appear, battered and furtive or out-and-out predatory. They fight and die of their wounds or go on to wander and fight and die somewhere else. Mostly, they withdraw to the abandoned lodges that fringe the dry edge of the marsh and feed upon their dead and upon the coarse weeds nearby. Old and young they are, the luckless, the footloose.

Life is cheapest among the young. In the more roomy areas, the weaned that are driven from lodges containing suckling young may find a measure of safety in empty lodges, coot nests, or dense vegetation, but, where small territory abuts small territory, the teeth of adults are readier to slash as well as harder to keep away from. Back and forth, from home lodges to neighbors' lodges, wary young slip ahead of and around the adults. Victims crawl upon rushy mats with their entrails hanging out or float with bodies softening in the heat. Four of five are dead before they are a third grown, some whole litters a fortnight after weaning; and the surviving young that live in odd corners or cluster around the more tolerant of the adults include animals that are both stunted and ailing.

The larger young eat of the fresher bodies, especially of the bodies of the very young and not always of bodies of young that are dead when found. Helpless litters in nests are also bitten to death by adults, and parents sometimes care for their own helpless young in the nests of other muskrat litters that they kill. Desertions of the new-born increase with the uneasiness and disturbances of crowding, as do losses from moving litter members from nest to nest. Breeding slackens and stops by midsummer, though continuing for weeks on less populated areas.

Out toward deep water, a food-rich frontier draws in the young that can reach it and a few of the old that live in the vicinity. It has dangers of its own, and some of the newcomers drown, but the vacant spaces where muskrats can live become filled to the rough and barren water of the center. Yet, most of the marsh-dwellers stay or try to stay where they are as long as that is the most comfortable thing to do—which is throughout the breeding season, or into late summer.

As might be expected, the breeding season is a period of pronounced tensions in our muskrat population. Reproduction of its kind is always among the most fundamental of responses of a living creature, with interplays of breeding-season intolerances. Hence, the behavior patterns of our muskrats become modified as late summer brings relief from the jealousies and frictions associated with mating and care of young. Food is then as plentiful as at any time of year, and the muskrats enjoy a freedom of movement that would not be tolerated during the main breeding season. The quarrelsome may still fight if they try, though transients are nearly all young animals that are neither formidable nor disposed to make trouble.

If our muskrat population is at all lucky from late summer on to the next spring's breeding season, it may live in relatively uneventful peace for several months—the earlier shaking down of the overproduced young having left the population in a position of some security. If the fall and winter weather remains favorable, if neither insufficient nor too much water covers the cattail and bulrush rootstocks, if the sinking frost-line does not encompass the food supply, the population may get along fairly well. There may be some chewed-up misfits wandering on the new ice of November or December or coming out later to be picked off by minks or foxes. In the spring, of course, a new breeding season and the birth of more young would again accentuate tensions in a crowded population.

Let us say that the muskrats of our marsh are *not* lucky, that, like some human populations, they have to meet a great emergency —an emergency aggravated by their already high densities and the limited alternatives open to them.

When the normal dryness of late summer or fall turns into drought on our muskrat marsh, there is still resilience in social relationships. The first young muskrats that drift into the marsh from surrounding potholes are tolerated the same as the local young that move inward from the drying shores after the breeding season. The big pinch does not come until the hard frosts bring in more wandering strangers and impress the residents with what they, themselves, are up against. One need not indulge in any anthropomorphizing to see that the muskrats recognize a change in their lives when they work to deepen their burrows beneath the frosted mud or travel back and forth between feeding grounds and ice-glazed waterholes or gnaw at exposed and frozen plant parts or sit by themselves with blood oozing from their fight wounds.

As winter approaches, strange muskrats meet with more and more hostility, whether they come from the borders of the marsh or from far outside. They gather in the weedy growths of low ground or spread along the shore. Wanderers are still mainly young ones, easily harassed into staying out of where they are not wanted, but among them are adults. Later, more adults—the last muskrats to abandon some of the long-dry, food-poor environment of the shore zone and outlying sloughs—work toward the deeper parts.

Some of these adults disregard established property rights. Some even kill and eat the less dangerous of the residents, moving from lodge to lodge until they die of their own wounds or from hunger and freezing, or the minks get them. They have raw or healing wounds on face or forelegs (perhaps a hamstrung foreleg, held on by the joint), two-inch gashes across rump, or hind feet or tails bitten through and swollen out of shape. They have abscesses the size of a golf ball under an armpit or bulging out a side, or a string of smaller abscesses running through the liver and the other organs of the body cavity, but, as long as their tough old bodies have life, they hang on to it.

A congested area on a drought-exposed marsh bottom need not be close to any main route of travel of evicted muskrats to be the scene of bloody crises. It need not suffer much invasion by muskrats coming from far outside. Where every stranger is a prospective enemy, taking or trying to take what it wants where it can find it, where viciously defended home ranges confront animals that want to go elsewhere or can find no real refuge anywhere, there we may not expect to find much peace in our muskrat population.

•   •   •

Let us consider our muskrat marsh during another year. We have about a quarter as many adult muskrats in early summer and a total number of adults and young after the breeding season that is perhaps only half as great as after the other breeding season. Food and water are much as before. The center is still rough and shelterless in stormy weather. The shallows still go dry in the fall. Minks range the borders, ready as ever to prey when they can. Things are about as before in all ways except for the fewer muskrats.

Our muskrats may still be said to have the attributes of muskrats in endeavoring to stay alive individually, to multiply, to exploit the marshes, to be more or less peaceable of temperament when comfortable and not aroused, and to be savage when uncomfortable and aroused.

In their own way, they may be called unimaginative, practical creatures, meeting slowly developing problems by default or by improvisions forced by patent crises. An alarming danger typically brings forth action, sometimes appropriate, sometimes inappropriate. The mental processes of the muskrats still function best when required to do but one thing at a time. The animals having the advantage in survival and competition are still the mature ones living in places where they have valid property rights. The psychology of dominant individuals is still of outstanding importance in the social order of the muskrat marsh.

Our marsh now still has muskrats that do not belong, troublemakers, wanderers, the ailing, the unlucky, the desperate. For all of that, there is little serious friction in the muskrat population, even at the height of a drought exposure. Many mothers give birth to three or four litters during the breeding season, and the young thrive in the cattails and bulrushes.

The big difference is in the degree of crowding to which the muskrats are subject and in the resilience with which those muskrats adjust both to population stresses and to emergencies. A population density half as great as a top-heavy one does not have its troubles reduced merely by half, in direct proportion to the numbers of muskrats present. Its gains, in social tranquility, are far out of proportion to the actual lowering of the population numerically.

Most important is the existence of shock-absorbing frontiers for the muskrats of the marsh and routes by which adjusting muskrats might reach them unimpeded, but greater day-by-day *Lebensraum* and comfortable conditions in the regularly maintained breeding territories also have their influence on the dispositions of the animals. Although modern evidence indicates that the psychological tolerances of the muskrats toward crowding may vary with the year as well as with circumstances, a safe generalization would appear to be that little peace can be expected in any population that acts as if it *feels* crowded.

The lives of muskrats cannot be thought to reflect more of human experience than man shares with other vertebrates rather generally. It would be absurd to expect the lives of muskrats and human experience to show parallels in great detail. Man, regardless of what else may be said of him, has demonstrated that he can complicate much of his living beyond comparison with much else, far beyond the complicating abilities of such simple eaters, breeders, fighters, and seekers after greener marshes as our muskrats.

Man seldom goes to such extremes as to rip open his progeny when they get annoyingly under foot. Outright cannibalism is not fashionable among civilized peoples. But the harshness of man toward man can equal anything to be seen on the marshes. It is not the way of muskrats to rationalize their cruder practices in terms of survival of the fittest or of manifest destiny or of chosen peoples or of utopian visions, but the common propensity of man and muskrats for growing savage under stress appears to be basic.

•   •   •

To me, overcrowding is so much the supreme factor underlying stress in the muskrat populations that its lessons may scarcely be overemphasized. It does function as a biological mechanism to reduce, in part, its own evils. Despite the rapidity with which the muskrats can multiply—even as rodents, they are among the more fecund—they are most productive of young at population densities that are neither extremely low nor extremely high for the environment occupied. This is a rule that seems to hold broadly true for other animal life. Moreover, populations of many species of animals show different degrees of self-limitation long before food competition reaches what are conventionally thought of as Malthusian stages. Without crediting to abstract reasoning these adjustments between reproductive potentials and problems of overpopulation, or ascribing to them more uniformity and effectiveness than exist, man should find it of interest that automatic, self-limiting adjustments occur.

Man should also find it of interest that the adjustments almost inevitably mean suffering in species capable of suffering. There is naturalness in them, whether the populations be of men or mice or muskrats, but the naturalness is that of life responding to harass-

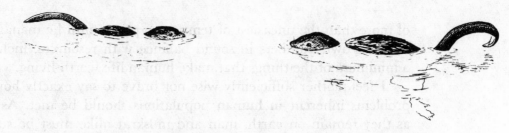

ment and frustration and necessity. What I have seen of Nature's way, in this respect, is the ruthless way, little resembling any mysteriously benign process of falling birth rates. Breeding may terminate painlessly with physiological changes at the end of a reproductive cycle, but, when a real self-limiting retrenchment in the normal reproductive pattern of a species possessed of a nervous system occurs, it is very apt indeed to be *forced* by something uncomfortable, if not ominous.

Being only lower animals, the muskrats may not be expected to teach man much about population behavior that is not elementary, but it is surprising—and frightening—how unaware influential people may be of the simpler biological backgrounds of sociology and economics during periods of crisis and political upheavals.

I have here attempted to sketch what should be regarded as a composite picture based upon factual evidence, based all the way through on known case histories of muskrat populations, every last bit of it. I have attempted to present a realistic portrayal of small scenes in the drama of life that may be conducive to more realistic human appraisals of some of the fundamentals underlying social relationships. In this, I recognize that I am coming close to the edge of controversial subjects that I am neither inclined nor competent to discuss. There remains for our thought the fidelity with which muskrats respond to inherent patterns, to resources, to the presence of other muskrats, to the presence of ancient enemies and to the interrelationships that may be observed in a natural society.

The principal moral that the lives of muskrats may have for us may be that the biological foundation of peace is that of moderation. This is admittedly a homely concept and not at all new. It is a concept having its own implications of unsolved problems when applied to human populations, not only of reconciling religious, political, and social differences, but also of actually defining the most enlightened and practical aims. It is a concept that man has a tendency to forget when he loses sight of the fact that he is an animal or when he imagines himself to be a higher, wiser, or more special animal than he is. I cannot see that man has any prospect

of marshes and the laws of life   149

of more than the uneasiest of temporary peace until he manages to keep his own numbers in sound balance with resources, including a minimum of the things that make human life worth living.

I feel neither sufficiently wise nor brave to say exactly how the problems inherent in human populations should be met. As long as they remain on earth, man and muskrat alike must be subject to some extent to blind forces which no amount of good judgment can completely offset. But man should be able to recognize the menace for his own kind that can build up with his own continued irresponsible increase in numbers, especially in our "atomic age" when what is precious in civilization cannot afford unnecessary risks of mass dislocations, mass agony, and mass desperation, with puppetry and puppet masters, and loss of human dignity, perhaps waiting just beyond.

At the very least, man should cease his obeisance to mere numbers. The merriment in the old saying, "the more the merrier," can become false as extremes are reached, even in such gregarious a species of animal as man can be.

•   •   •   •

Whether a person thinks of the inconceivable millions of stars, each so much greater than our whole earth, or of only muskrats, or of anything else in Nature that is either greater or lesser than he is, a feeling of humility before the Order that exists in the universe is always appropriate. If disturbed at the parallels between mankind and nonhuman societies, he may be reminded that no man invented life's rules of behavior. They have been in operation for a long time. They will continue to be operative.

The philosophy that man should "work with and not against Nature" may have interpretations differing with the individual or the group, but, in its broader senses, it seems acceptable to enlightened people just about everywhere. Whatever may be the emotional hazards of differing metaphysical and political beliefs, "working with Nature" implies avoidance of misconceptions as to the nature of Nature and, going further, some faculty for choice between wise and unwise alternatives. The lessons as well as the beauties of marshes await the perceptive, as do the lessons and beauties of the skies, of the seas, of the mountains, and of the other places remaining where man can still reflect upon lessons and beauties that are not of human making.